A WALK IN THE DARK AGES

Frank Delaney is a well-known radio and television broadcaster. He originated and presented the award-winning Radio Four series 'Bookshelf', hosted his own BBC2 series, and has made many documentary contributions to the BBC, including 'The Celts', a six-part series screened on BBC1 in 1987, the book of which was published the previous year. His earlier books, *James Joyce's Odyssey* and *Betjeman Country*, occupied prominent places on the bestseller lists. A native of southern Ireland, he lives in London.

Items

in the

A WALK
IN THE
DARK AGES

FRANK DELANEY

FONTANA/Collins

First published in Great Britain by
William Collins Sons & Co. 1988
First issued in Fontana Paperbacks 1990

Copyright © Genesis Productions Ltd 1988
Text copyright © Frank Delaney 1988

Designed and produced by
Genesis Productions Ltd
30 Great Portland Street
London WIN 5AD

Design and original drawings by
Christos Kondeatis
Picture research by Gabrielle Allen

Printed and bound in Great Britain by
William Collins Sons & Co., Glasgow

To my son, Frank

ACKNOWLEDGEMENTS

The author wishes to make the following acknowledgements to those who have assisted him directly, or otherwise facilitated the writing of this book:

Gabrielle Allen, whose diligent picture research surmounted difficult traditional obstacles; Cambridge Computers, who facilitated the use of the Z88 portable computer on which much of the notes and travel research were written and recorded, and who assisted in the interfacing with an Apple SE; Marjory Chapman at William Collins, who gave thoughtful encouragement; Thomas Charles-Edwards at Corpus Christi College, Oxford, for assistance in consideration of the social background to Irish *peregrinatio*; Jim Cochrane and Jeremy Cox of Genesis Productions, who conceived the idea in the first place and who gave unstinting and patient support; Ian Hill, for valiant efforts to secure safe passage from the Antrim coast to Iona; the historian Edward James at the University of York, who unselfishly gave access to his own work, and offered valuable suggestions; Christos Kondeatis and Jane Ewart, who designed the book; my agent Michael Shaw at Curtis Brown/John Farquharson; and Susan Collier, who shared much of the journey.

Thanks are also due to the following for permission to use quotations:

Jonathan Cape Ltd and the Estate of Cecil Day-Lewis for permission to quote from the translations of Virgil's *Eclogues*; John Montague for permission to quote from 'Colmcille' translated by John Montague; Miss Mary Margaret Martin of Kilmacrew House, Banbridge, County Down, Northern Ireland and Dame Felicitas Corrigan and the Community of Stanbrook Abbey, Worcester for permission to quote from the writings of Helen Waddell.

CONTENTS

THE ROUTE OF
THE LATTER-DAY
PILGRIM

No such accurate route maps as these existed in the seventh
century, and although the Romans measured in lengths rather than
days a traveller in the Dark Ages had few precise concepts
of distance. The pilgrim journey of this book both crossed and
followed trade routes of the times – those which were usually
taken for safety and expediency by migrants, soldiery,
international legations and other travellers. Pilgrims did not,
however, always adhere to their planned route, but might
take detours for reasons such as illness, religious worship, bad
weather, or to visit a shrine or a famous abbot.

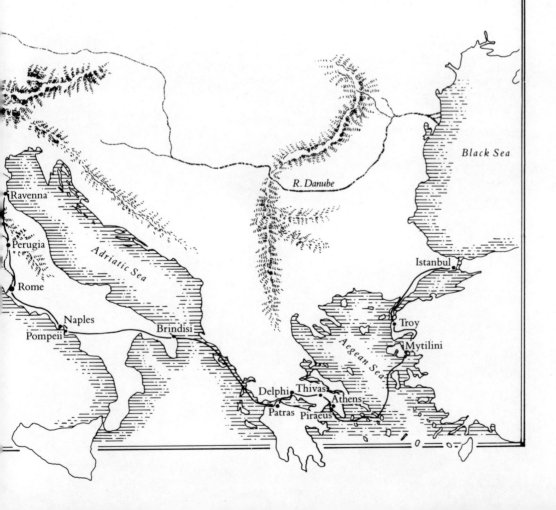

PREFACE

TRAVEL THROUGH EUROPE has become a novelty of reducing value. The old enterprise attached to visiting Rome if you were a cleric, the fashionable *cachet* of taking the Grand Tour if you were socially eager, have disappeared. Few new journeys may be made, no new ground can be broken. The dimensions of distance, means of travel and geographical accessibility have all been brought under control. We have little left by way of adventure.

Except ... except the elements of time and the imagination: we can make journeys which have to do with the past, hunting Medicis in Florence, visualizing what Guidobaldo's court at Urbino must have felt like, measuring in educated guesses the life of the people of Herculaneum.

The journey of this book, from the harsh rock of Skellig Michael to the – equally, but differently – harsh city of Istanbul, certainly had physical travel in it: every moment of the way was covered. It had, however, much more to do with time and the imagination than with travel in the intrepid sense. No dangers lay in my way greater than, at either extreme, wet socks or sunburn: beyond a few clerks, juggernauts and hotel managers, no beasts threatened my pathway. Yet the sense of adventure never dimmed, and it became a true voyage of discovery – not because I had never travelled such a route before; indeed I already knew many of the places thoroughly – but because the light in which I was seeing everything had changed.

One of the emblems of early European travel portrayed a monk, upright and hopeful, walking the long roads of Europe with staff and satchel – a pilgrim to a holy place, walking in the Dark Ages to Rome or Santiago de Compostela or Tours. He cut a necessarily puny, none the less interesting figure, a dot on the landscape, in his awkward robe with his unbecoming appearance, dishevelled, that curious haircut, a little wild perhaps, or unsettlingly saintly. He had his reasons for travelling – genuine prayer and preaching, or – one of the farther reaches of self-denial – self-imposed exile in the service of God, or penance. He had his place, too: the wandering monk, especially if he had learning – and whether he travelled alone or in a group of fellows, a mobile monastery in search of a site, like bees looking for a hive – contributed an as yet unmeasured wedge of culture to the shifting jigsaw that became Europe.

My travels sought to follow the seeker, to discover such a monk on his voyage of discovery. I would look at the sights he saw, try and view them as he viewed them, balance the impressions against the facts of my own existence. That, in theory, was my intention. The facts of the journey, however, often put me down on shores and hillsides which had not changed since the seventh century, and in truth, and many times quite rightly, I found myself as bewildered as he must have been, and with no option but to work out the implications – for myself as well as for this figure through whose eyes I had set out to look.

Even though I began by inventing such a man – to establish a physical presence, for the purposes of keeping an eye on him – the fiction of him, like the composite technique used by any novelist creating characters, came from fact. He therefore became real, and feasibly so, and although no traceable individual made this precise geographical journey, many hundreds, perhaps thousands, walked different stages of it and were known to have done so.

Since we do not necessarily know all there is to be known about the fictional, any more than the real, characters of our acquaintance, I have taken care not to state my monk's spiritual purpose. That must remain unknown, his business entirely. Maybe he merely wanted to pray, with a little evangelizing. Perhaps he had doubts about his faith, queries which pushed him towards Constantinople, to ask what lay behind this burning light called Islam. The factual men who went before him, and whose names – Columba, Gallus, Columbanus – remain enshrined in the ecclesiastical and secular history of the Dark Ages, usually intended to spread the word of the Christian God, while gaining their own salvation, as their faith instructed them to do. I did give the monk whose road I followed a purpose they could never have had (except unwittingly and much later as historians tracked them down). I made him my pathfinder on a purely personal – selfish, if you like – expedition whose greatest end was knowledge and discovery, whose lesser aim was the pleasure of travel, shifting on from town to town. By gazing at the sights and places he must have seen, and in many cases could not have avoided, my own learning, the permanent state of being educated, would be assisted. In my imagination I followed at a distance behind this decent and gentle man of the cloth, trying to see what he saw thirteen hundred years ago, and without the benefit of a historian's training, trying to survey and to judge the life and times of his world.

Although the year of his great journey, AD 687, was chosen for the obvious reason of being a straightforward thirteen centuries ago from the time I embarked, it had other factors to recommend it. By the seventh century the Church had established itself sufficiently to accommodate such a wandering monk, a man equipped with enough education and social experience of other such travellers to allow him to contemplate such a journey. He held some language in common to ease his task: he certainly had at least a slim knowledge of Latin, from his texts and from the written communications of Rome and the bishops. The Church to which he belonged had developed a clear and muscular identity, emerging as a world power with experience of all the divisions and schisms necessary to the growing process of any movement with an intellectual dimension. The continent of Europe stood at perhaps its most turbulent juncture politically, as the terms of reference of old empires and new invaders shifted and swung. Cultures collapsed, the vacuums they left began to fill again; laws changed, borders disappeared or were redrawn – all happening with what seems, in history's telescope, bewildering speed. Full record of the new had not, by a long chalk, begun to be kept, and at the same time the whitening relics of the old, the pagan and the classical, could still be seen and felt. It soon became apparent to me, an eager, amateur enquirer, that it must have been one of the most exciting periods Europe has ever known – and one of the most difficult to capture.

The terms of reference I gave myself – to regard, insofar as I could, the Europe that such a monk of the Dark Ages would have seen – proved impossible to keep. The record of the period too often proved too slim, and parameters of a century either side, or sometimes deeper consideration of the periods before him, frequently became necessary. The attraction of choosing as Dark an Age as possible also became the frustration. Time after time the longing to know just that little bit more – the wish that somebody, somewhere, in a house of Lombardy, or an office in Greece, had kept a journal – became almost unbearable. In the end I had to settle for the feel of the period above the minute facts, for the atmosphere and possibilities of the age above the specific documented moment – which did not, after all, exist, hence the term 'Dark' Ages. In fact this limitation enhanced, rather than crippled, the aspect of the journey most vital to me – the imaginative element.

The journey achieved its end – and merrily defeated it. As required, it opened out the era for me – and smartly told me how little it opened it out, thereby threatening to send me off on all sorts of future journeys, on further searches for the Merovingians and the Franks and their jewelled cicadas, for the musicians who wrote the hymn annotation at Delphi, for the fictional possibilities in Theodora, the whore who became Empress of Constantinople. It sent me searching, too, for the monk himself, to whom I so often stood so near, chagrined at myself for allowing what essentially began as a travel book to turn so riskily towards obsessive preoccupation, because it did, on another level, turn into a personal journey, out of darkness into light. I may have left him standing on a street in Constantinople, but I will go on wondering what is to become of him, which is not a fit occupation for any traveller, armchair or otherwise.

Essentially the result stays close to its planned original identity – a travel book whose intention was to make a journey of the imagination as well as of the body. Such voyages, made in an effort to refresh the variations of modern travelling through Europe, offer possibilities: why not trace a soldier in Napoleon's army, or a centurion in Caesar's, a manservant in a prince's entourage or a secretary in a merchant's wagon train? Time and our imagination have, after all, a large part to play in the difficult business of history, where point of view has as much importance as fact.

In the end it comes down to escape, and why should it not? Stalking, at a respectable distance, this monk in his robe as he went looking for a cave on a Scottish headland, or walking not far behind him through a lantern-lit fair in Lincoln, or across a hill in the Marne valley had the same quality of escape as a novel or a film. He became real, often, and almost dragged me off course once or twice, almost made me stay longer than I should have in places that he found important, and made me wonder on many occasions whose book it was. That was, of course, the whole idea – that I should follow him cheerfully, in a spirit of enquiry, and with a great deal more comfort than he had, and that the whole enterprise should result in a vicarious relationship of three tiers – monk, writer and reader. I can only render an account of the first two.

Frank Delaney
London
Summer 1988

I wish, O Son of the Living God, O ancient, eternal King,
For a little hidden hut in the wilderness that it may be my dwelling.

An all-grey little lake to be by its side
A clear pool to wash away sins through the grace of the Holy Spirit.

Quite near, a beautiful wood around it on every side,
To nurse many-voiced birds, hiding it with its shelter.

A southern aspect for warmth, a little brook across its floor,
A choice land with many gracious gifts such as to be good for every plant.

This is the husbandry I would take, I would choose, and will not hide it;
Fragrant leek, hens, speckled salmon, trout, bees.

Raiment and food enough for me from the King of fair fame,
And I to be sitting for a while praying God in every place.

'The Prayer of Mauchan'
from the Gaelic: early monastic,
between seventh and tenth century

CHAPTER ONE

HERE IS GOD, IF YOU LIKE

JUST AFTER DAWN on a summer morning in AD 687, a robed figure descended the side of an island rock out in the Atlantic. From the summit he trod down the steep irregular levels, moving resolutely, though wary of his foothold; a calm morning, no breeze, not a ripple on the ocean. If seen from the distance he could be picked out, a small moving figure, made conspicuous against the darker surroundings of the rock by his garment of rough off-white wool.

The descent took almost an hour. He stopped from time to time and gazed over the edges of the cliffs at the shelves of seabirds in their vertical tenements; they had just begun to clear their throats for the first huge chorus of the day. A gannet dived. As it hit the water its wings closed so fast he could not follow the movement. The bird completed the shallow underwater trajectory in the calm green sea and came up swallowing a fish.

Above, on the summit of the rock, the monks whose raw but devout community he was departing had already been in prayer for some hours, rising at two in the morning for the first of the many daily devotions. Through the oratory window the other rock came into view, handmaid in shape and respectful distance to this great monastery crag. The small Skellig whitened in the dawn with the flocks and flocks of birds.

He continued his descent to the lower reaches, carrying a small parcel of food, bread wrapped in cloth. As he reached the cove and the water's edge, he looked back up the pathway of his descent and saw another white-robed figure descending more rapidly than he had done – another monk, who would row him ashore.

From here the cliffs rose sheer and hard and black, straight above his head, with grass and green fronds glistening with damp. St Michael had promised that nobody who came on pilgrimage should fail to make the crossing from the mainland safely – but had he said anything about getting back again? The tribe of monks who stayed here all the year round aged rapidly, their faces gouged by the fasting and the weather, and calmed by their meditations.

In the distance the thin line of light marking out the coastline had brightened and the mainland could now be seen clearly. The two men lifted the skin coracle from the cranny which sheltered it in the boulders, carried it to the water, set it down and climbed in. Facing the bow, the rower picked up the wooden rowing staves, handed one to the monk behind him and began to work the other, bobbing about until they got the coracle under control. The small rock, soon coming up on their immediate left, had a population of seals sitting around the base, brownish and blackish, with interested, old, wise, pleasant faces, like monks themselves. Above them, the white birds and their guano covered the rest of the rock like snow.

In the noon sunshine the two men landed on a small beach. The rower held the boat steady until the parcel of food had been lifted clear, took a warm leave with many blessings, and then set off again, back to Skellig Michael. The monk sat down on the sand and began to eat his bread. From this excellent vantage point, the slight haze rendered the two rocks sailing out in the ocean even more mystic. The only noise came from the small waves and larksong; behind him, in the empty land, not a sight nor a soul.

I stood on the top of Skellig Michael on a summer afternoon, trying to visualize the departure from this rock of such a monk – and his life here, the weather, the hardship and the emotional pressures. I had gone to the

Skelligs from Valentia island, on Des Lavelle's boat. He descends from five generations of Valentia islanders, and three generations of lighthouse keepers.

'What is it, Des? About the Skelligs? Why does the place captivate people?'

Not a pick of flesh on him, rangy and tanned and reserved, with a natural exquisiteness of language.

'I don't know. I suppose it's the … it's the … the soul of the place.'

Searching for words. He has a shrewd face, without cunning or guile, and is possessed of instinctive courtesy and intelligence beyond the reaches of formal education.

'No other message that is written or spoken can convey the same message. To me at any rate. Here is God, if you like.'

His life revolves exactly and metaphorically around the Skelligs. In the winter he lectures across America on the phenomenal nature and presence of the two Skelligs rocks, catalogues his photographs, plans forthcoming private visits, wildlife vigils and diving journeys into the 250-foot depths, pursuing his obsession as the Skelligs' most sedulous recorder. In the summer he ferries boatloads of travellers, such as our motley pilgrim caravan, from Britain and Europe, from other parts of Ireland. We had a pair of priests, a young couple, six pupils with their teacher and two local folk who had lived within sight of the Skelligs all their lives but had never gone there.

Five boats sat anchored at the jetty of Portmagee, one a small French yacht, the others local lobster boats; Valentia once commanded the transatlantic cable to America. The Skelligs boatmen travel down a long sound, and by Bray Head they hit the ramp of the Atlantic swell. Sometimes the boatmen refuse to leave the pier, even though the sea and the morning seem perfectly calm. The foam and the tide on nearer stretches of the coastline can tell them whether an attempted landing on the rock will succeed. Skellig Michael has one, highly vulnerable landing place. Query their reluctance to sail and, full of experience and local precision, they will tell you that on 27 December 1955 a wave took out the Skelligs lighthouse, 175 five feet up.

'The volume of the place' – Des Lavelle stood in the wheelhouse, about to turn on the engine – 'the sheer magnificence of it, would strike everyone, it must do. Even people who have a preconceived idea of the place, who have read about it, may even have seen a slide programme or two, it still strikes them. This is bigger than humanity, if you like.'

The waves could hardly be calmer, no sea-legs required. They say you can see porpoises and the occasional school of whales in these waters, and the emperor butterfly borne over from the Americas in the jet slipstreams.

Skellig Michael from the air.

We trembled a little, no more than that, as the waters of the sound folded us over into the Atlantic.

Blind Man's Cove has been smoothed with concrete. Climbing from the boat none the less requires concentration; the slightest swell out there in the ocean would make the landing in this cove impossible. In the television series *Civilization*, Lord Clark argued that in the Dark Ages western European culture clung on by the fingernails at the Skellig, and in similar settlements, where the monks kept thought and art alive.

Des Lavelle pointed out above us the outlines of old steps, thought by some – and feasibly so – to be the route by which the early hermits ascended: dangerous now though, and officially ruled out of bounds. In any case we would have needed a long ladder to reach the first of them, so we took the broad tarred way to the lighthouse.

They lived here in all weathers, a tribe of fishers. The anchorites of the desert, whose tradition these monks pursued, selected locations where the force of their veneration was driven on by nature in the raw. 'To this spot', says the *Vitae Patrum*, an anthology of the words of the Desert Fathers, 'those who have had their first initiation and who desire to live a remoter life, stripped of all its trappings, withdraw themselves: for the desert is vast, and the cells are sundered from one another by so wide a space that none is in sight of his neighbour, nor can any voice be heard. One by one they abide in their cells, a mighty silence and a great quiet among them....' Here, on the Skellig, that early eastern tradition of the desert hermit, and the ensuing Christian tradition of the monk, merged. The remote Irishmen also lived in cells, but nearer to each other and with a closer sense of community.

By looking up, you can see how they first survived on Skellig Michael, sheltering in the lees of the great crags, and then moving upwards to slightly more benign terrain. They ate seabirds, whose meat a later visitor described as 'fishy and rank'. At Cross Cove, the roadway turns a hairpin into a cauldron of noise so loud you have to raise your voice to be heard. Over the low wall you can touch the nests of the guillemots and the fulmars and the kittiwakes, in their perilous niches, descending straight down the cliffs to the water's edge. The noise rises in a constant edgy surge, screeching and screaming, with 'kitti-wake, kitti-wake, kitti-wake' dominant. Feathers, and sometimes an egg, tumble down, way down, into the green waters. Further on, the ground cover teems with variety, mosses and lichens and small plants and little bright pink flowers, fed with dampness from fissures in the rocks, gathered rainwater, or mysterious springs.

Beyond the noisy, feathered, high density of Cross Cove, broad and considered steps lead up to the right; some of the slabs must weigh half a ton. People in Waterville, on the mainland coast, had said, 'Be sure and count the steps.' According to tradition, nobody knows the exact number of steps up to the monastery, and visitors, confused with the wonder and holiness of the place – 'Here is God, if you like' – never remember whether it was 593, or 538, or 584. Neither did I.

To the north-east behind us lay the long line of coast we had left. To the north-west lay those low islands, the clusters of rocks, towards which Ir, the son of Mil, rowed so hard that he collapsed and died within sight of landfall, and thus gave his name to the shore he never gained, 'Ir-land'; instead he found a rocky grave on the Skellig. To the south and west you will find nothing save sky and green ocean between here and the coast of Brazil. At Christ's Saddle, beneath the Needle's Eye, the rock's highest point, 714 feet above the sea, I turned right, climbing upwards on the last of the broad steps, out of breath.

Since boyhood, I have been tramping the ruins of abbeys; their skeletal cloisters have always drawn me in, regardless of their state of preservation. Some stood directly by the roadside, or far in the depths of fields, glimpsed through trees from small by-roads, the bicycle flung suddenly behind the ditch. Now on Skellig Michael, a farm of stones, I had never seen a monastery garden so small, and so unelaborate; no medieval choirs of nightingales here, yet the simple walls and their jagged edges immediately offered more peace than any other holy place of my acquaintance. Just ahead, through a short 'tunnel' to the terrace, camouflaged in the harvest of rocks, stood several tall igloos of stone.

These buildings have received generous care. The settlement has been restored to its six cells of dry stone, shaped like beehives. The floor of each cell has a roughly quadrangular shape; as the building rises, the walls curve gently inward to form the dome of the beehive. The stone smells a little musty, friendly, and the way in which the ascending stones softly overlap each other adds to the warmth.

As the courses of stones were laid from the ground upwards, each circle of walling advanced in upon the previous one, with each stone projecting a little further inward, overlapping the one on which it rested. This building system – known as 'corbelling', from the way in which the upper beak of the raven, the Latin *corvus*, the French *corbeau*, the Scots *corby*, overlaps the lower – progressed serenely upward until eventually, when all the courses had moved closer and closer to the centre of the circle, the remaining gap could be sealed with a single stone. No mortar was used, no plaster, no masonry; nothing but the grey-beige stones, dry with surface dust.

The cells have a roomy tranquillity, with walls almost six feet thick, and

– surprisingly, given how small they seem on the outside – no sense of cramp, or confined space. Some pegs for hanging clothes still project from the walls; you can still see the shelves and cupboards of the monks. Nobody has inhabited these for many, many centuries. Sunlight walks through the narrow doorway, and inside the hearts of the cell walls small birds have made their nests; they lie there and cheep drowsily. Emerging from the cells, every monk who ever lived here saw the full spectacle of the place, vastnesses of sky and ocean, every morning of his life.

A few steps away, past the well which dries up, they say, at the sound of blasphemy, the oratory window, oriented liturgically to the east, also happens to frame the small Skellig. This tiny chapel was built on the same corbelled principle, though rectangular rather than circular, and the finished effect resembles an upturned boat. The ancient builders picked out, with playgroup simplicity, one or two small quartz-flecked crosses in the stonework. Occasionally a priest from the mainland celebrates Mass here; the legend of St Michael says that the altar wine never runs out and never needs replenishing.

In the churchyard, among a small cluster of other ancient stones, all crude, some fallen, some leaning, one cross stood out. It had rays cut into it, radiating out from the centre as if in echo of ancient sun worship; it would not have surprised me to find it in a Mexican forest or a South American temple. Perhaps the pagan hermits carved it, before the Christian monks came, although it also suggested the familiar configuration of the later Celtic cross, the arms of the cruciform held within a circle, an image which has always conjured for me a holy man standing against the sun with his arms stretched out in prayer.

Occasional mares' tails of cloud drifted across the blue sky. During rough weather, though, the spray from the waves can drench the Needle's Eye far above the beehive huts. In various nooks and crannies around and about the monastery, runs of ground showed traces of reclamation from the bare rock, trenches made, filled with good clay brought from elsewhere and then fenced against the wind. Up here the wind can knock a man forward, the rain drives and drives into every pocket in the skin. The rock has unsafe cliff edges, boulders which slip and topple, and the ocean below completes the gang of dangers, clutching higher, ripping away. Countering these forces, total silence frequently falls. On a calm night, the only noise comes from the occasional shuffle of a puffin or the swish of a petrel.

I had received rare permission to stay overnight on the rock, sharing the sleeping quarters of the lighthouse men, ferried nowadays by helicopter. About ten o'clock, in darkness, I left the lighthouse and climbed the steps back up to the monastery walls. Nothing moved. I found myself reciting all the words I could think of in the English language to hold in suspense a

High Cross at Clonmacnoise, County Offaly.

quieter moment than I had experienced for years. All failed, none of them adequate.

I walked back down the pathway for mugs of tea and talk of shipwrecks. Mainland folklore claims that the Atlantic Ocean flows deepest round the Skelligs, and that the two rocks once formed part of Macgillicuddy's Reeks, Ireland's highest mountain range. In the lives of those who see it daily from the mainland, Skellig always had a presence. Easter came later to Skellig Michael, they said, than to the mainland; perhaps this echoed the liturgical disturbances of the seventh century, culminating in the Synod of Whitby in 664, where the Roman timing of Easter finally took precedence over the Celtic Church's interpretation.

I had set the alarm clock to wake me at four and catch the dawn. Instead, I woke naturally – the silence, I think – and as the dark began to lighten, climbed for the third time to the beehive cells. Again, not a puff of wind, not a noise, peacefully and utterly silent. I had a tape recorder with me, a Uher 4000, a professional machine. I turned it to 'Record'. Hardly a flicker showed on the needle; the machine displayed almost no sign of recording anything, as if no sound was taking place. When I played it back later I could hear no more than the mildest atmosphere. In a few moments this changed beautifully as a wren, perched on the sun cross just before me, opened up and sang hard for the next hour in the clement light.

The morning grew warm and the rock could be explored before the boat came back. On a far, high corner, a pilgrim pathway called the Stations of the Cross demands a rigorous nerve. It ends in a long, narrow stone overhang at the Needle's Eye, out along which the pilgrim must crawl, 700 feet above the foam, kiss the cross carved into the rock, and return.

I understand Des Lavelle's obsession with the place. He sees the Skelligs in the distance almost every day of his life, holy mirages, mountains of the local moon.

'Even on a calm day the potential is here for power. For destruction. The sea. And the wind of course, the gales. And another thing – these waters were the trade routes, even in the most ancient times. So we're sitting here at the crossroads of our roots. With all that power. I've been here in the winter. You should see a winter storm.'

On the last step downwards, the birds flocked around and about, the puffins looking tailored and inquisitive, and the white javelins of the gannets piercing the waters. We left in the early afternoon.

The monk whose fictitious, composite path I wanted to trace had set out only for Columba's Iona. Intending to follow in the footprints he would have made if he had left the Skellig rock and journeyed from shrine to shrine in search of wider enlightenment, I intended to fetch up in the city once called Constantinople, which was then, according to its emperors, 'the centre of the known world', confluence of East and West. By means of abbeys and ancient sites, my map references would be, wherever possible, seventh-century places which the monk would have stayed in or passed through.

Transfixing contrasts lay ahead – between origin and destination, beween the corbelled beehive cells of Skellig Michael and the minarets of Istanbul, between the empty rock of this retreat and the bright, busy waters of the Golden Horn. In 675, Bishop Arculf in Iona (on a pilgrimage in the opposite direction) gave the Abbot Adamnan a detailed description of the founding of Constantinople. The Emperor Constantine, after a dream, led a procession to mark out the boundary, and he walked and walked – much farther than his attendants had anticipated. Eventually, in answer to their enquiries, he replied, 'I shall still advance until He, the invisible guide who marches before me, thinks proper to stop.' The modern measurement of Skellig Michael suggests an area of forty-four acres, most of it inaccessible.

The boat, which doubles as a trawler or a lobster boat, pushed away from Blind Man's Cove. The spray came over the deck on the way back to Valentia. The crowded galleries of birds on the small Skellig stood shoulder to shoulder, no room for an extra feather. Soon, like hands over the ears, the sound leading to Portmagee closed in about us.

The unknown builders of those stone beehives, so generous with their peace and with the vision they bequeathed, could have been in the Andes, or on an Asian mountain, or in a dream. Hours later, from high up the pass on the Dingle peninsula, I looked back for a last view of the two rocks as their peaks drifted into a mist.

Out to the west the Blasket islands lay in sunlight, a secret world which until earlier this century still held the traces of a people both neolithic and imaginative, with stories probably current before Christ. On that Dingle shore, for instance, near the village of Ventry, Daragh Donn, the Brown Oak, who was King-of-all-the-World-except-Ireland, tried to subjugate the people, and he suffered a great defeat at the hands of the mighty Finn McCool. Ireland's monks built the beginnings of a literature on the back of such stories, founded upon a clear folk culture. The history of the land since the earliest times took the form of epic tales – of travel, faraway places, exotic names, part legend, part fancy, part fact. Early record and pseudo-history, such as *The Annals of Innisfallen*, fused mythological, biblical and Christian themes and told, for example, how the sons of Mil, a Scythian ruler who died in Spain, eventually arrived at the shores of Ireland, *en route* from Scythia.

[They were] three months at sea until they reached Pharaoh, king of Egypt. They remained seven years with Pharaoh in Egypt ... Scotta, Pharoah's daughter, married Mil, son of Bile, in the eighth year. Pharaoh was drowned subsequently with his host in the Red Sea .... They voyaged after that around Scythia to the entrance to the Caspian Sea. They anchored twenty-seven days in the Caspian Sea by reason of the singing of the mermaids until Caicher the Druid delivered them. Caicher the Druid said to them 'Until we reach Ireland we shall not halt.'

Other tales, current in these parts when Christianity washed over Ireland in the fifth century, told of Persians and tribes of Babylon, of Haman and Cyrus, son of Darius, and Abraham. When missionaries returned from monasteries in Britain and on the continent they supplemented the romance with exotic names, prayers and descriptions of faraway kingdoms. With this new information, added to the aeons of oral mythology, Ireland laid the foundations of a great early literature.

Through the mountain passes I headed for Killarney. Further up through Ireland, the land becomes less stony, more lush.

> The splendour falls on castle walls,
> And snowy summits old in story;
> The long light shakes across the lakes,
> And the wild cataract leaps in glory.

High above Ladies' View, the panorama for which people have wanted to buy Killarney, the rain came down across the mountains and blotted out the long light of Tennyson's lakes. My paternal ancestors belong near here, and lived through the Famine, the Great Hunger, of the nineteenth century. Only sparse living ever came from this earth: one blow of the spade, my father said, and the sparks flew off the rock beneath the clay. Yet the vegetation in the woods blooms huge and luxuriant, with great leaves, brilliant, strange flowers, and the damp plush of large mosses; the Gulf Stream comes right up the Kenmare River and encourages these growths.

From the coast I had left, home of St Fionan the Crooked from Derrynane, or St Fionan the Leper from Ballinskelligs, and all along this countryside, early holy men had found niches for themselves in crags and caves and hollows in the mountains, or clearings in the woods. They went on their solitary way before the monastic idea was well established, with neither scrip nor scrap, the principle of the arid desert. Let us not get carried away with the notion that all those who grew to monkish stature did so out of zeal and the love of God. Many fled life, for reasons of crime or eccentricity or madness or weakness or other unacceptability, or the liberty to practise psychologically doubtful rituals such as self-denial on a violent scale, or self-inflicted corporal punishment.

In truth, the legends often overwhelmed the fact – which may have been intentional, since much of their performance of sanctity had a bravura quality. Simeon of Antioch, in the fifth century, raised his platform from ten feet to sixty feet above the ground and prostrated himself 'ten dozen times a day'. He came down by ladder for ceremonial and political events; otherwise he communicated by means of a basket raised and lowered. He also offered to passers-by, in the course of his thirty-seven years on the perch, cures for infertility and impotence.

Some of these early religious – including the Irish – came from families who had no place for them, who cast them out, left them to wander and mutter. Others had gone on the run from their own temptations, like the fourth-century Jerome, in the desert.

Every day tears, every day sighing: and if in spite of my struggles sleep would tower over and sink upon me, my battered body ached on the naked earth. Of food and drink I say nothing, since even a sick monk uses only cold water, and to take anything cooked is wanton luxury. Yet that same I, who for fear of hell condemned myself to such a prison, I, the comrade of scorpions and wild beasts, was there, watching the maidens in their dances: my face haggard with fasting, my mind burned with desire in my frigid body . . . .

For those so tempted and for those cast out, the development of the anchorite tradition still came as an awkward kind of godsend – shelter, community of sorts, no responsibilities and a licence to be egregious. Anchorites were granted full permission to visit outrage upon their person, and eventually admiration of a kind – that such worship could be so intense – could only come to mean that they were actually chosen by God. The life in the stone cells which they scattered through these hills decreed hardship, privation, cold, damp and loneliness. I have been in these mountains at night, in rain, in fog; all notion of hospitality disappears. The black light of the night shines on the lakes and a wind comes down through the crags and takes the skin off your lips.

Beyond here, going north, the land improves. Kerry's tradition of poverty led Patrick to bless the county from its borders, evading the need to travel through. The place of my next signpost, Emly, fared much better – prosperous country, where, according to some sources, *The Annals of Innisfallen* were written in a monastery founded by St Ailbe. Five centuries after the death of Christ, the ancestors of this society received the evangelists bringing Latin and the faith which would pervade the island – first Palladius, sent by Pope Celestine to minister to 'the Irish who believe in Christ', and later the former slave from Britain, Patrick. They also brought with them Greco-Roman ideas and ethics – if not fully observed or put into practice, at least in sufficient presence to cause some impact. Early trade with France encouraged the monastic idea, seen in Tours and similar establishments. When it got well under way, in the sixth and seventh centuries, the monastic system offered much to Irish society: respectability, social stability, a consolidation of the local kingship – since many of the abbeys became extensions of the tribe – as well as a source of learning.

The young monks, who filled the monasteries to overflowing, were required to perform the many physical labours of the community – the tending of the animals, the sowing and harvesting – and in the *scriptorium* they made books, needed to further the education of the monks and to add to the worship. These contained sacred writings, scriptures and psalms, in Latin, as well as local and national genealogies and annals of the countryside. Some took the form of plain and direct entries, some became beautifully decorated.

One distinguished strand ran through their worship. The seeds of Christianity in Ireland had fallen into an earth fertilized by centuries of natural worship. The 'pagans' believed in tree gods and water goddesses, in mountains and animals and sunlight. When combined, the new faith and the old belief gave Irish Christianity a unique flavour.

Late that morning I drove into the Golden Vale, a broad fertile seam which runs across part of the counties of Cork, Limerick and Tipperary, the sparkling waistband of the province of Munster. Easy to see why the love of nature persisted and played as much a part in the worship of their God as the imported Latin rite. Rich land here, on the borders of Limerick and Tipperary, long valleys of loam and timber. Thirteen hundred years ago, woods of oak and box and myrtle crowned these hills, and large lakes flooded the countryside. In these ancient parishes neighbours of the Dark Ages arrived by boat.

As they wrote about 'many-voiced birds' and 'speckled salmon', the monks of the *scriptorium* also called upon nature for the practical end of their trade. They used quills made of badger hairs and the tail-brushes of squirrels, they made dyes and inks from vegetables and wild herbs. Their manuscripts included the figures from these small wild kingdoms.

The storytellers say that long before the Bible was written the giant, Finn McCool, hunted over this land and heard 'the music of what happens', which he described as 'the sweetest sound in all the world'. By the shoulder of the Galtee Mountains the signposts had enticing names – Anglesborough, Ballylanders and Galbally; in the distance squatted the small sloping range of hills known as Slieve na Muck, the Hill of the Pigs, where Patrick turned a horde of devils into swine, and I had approached from the south-east the village of Emly, the first actual foretaste of monkish Europe.

Emly, Gaelic name Imleach Iubhair, the city of St Ailbe, forms the other half of the archdiocese of Cashel and Emly, one of the four pillars of Irish Catholicism. Emly has been important, say its people, since 1900 BC (difficult to establish quite how they calculate that date). Ptolemy called Emly one of the three principal centres of Ireland. According to the earliest legends – preferred locally – Ailbe preceded those first evangelists, Palladius the Gaul in 431, and, in the following year, Patrick. Time was when any such suggestion would have come close to Irish heresy. None the less, part of Irish teaching now accepts that Patrick may only have been the most powerful evangelist, the most – dare one say it? – publicized.

The legend of Ailbe begins with the name: Imleach Iubhair means the 'land of yew trees bordering on the lake'. A few miles from here, where the lake began, in Knockainey ('the hill of Aine', a goddess of the moon), lived Olencus, a courtier at the local kingship of Cronan. According to the biographical documents of Ailbe in Salamanca, young Olencus fell in love with a woman of the household – an unsuitable match, older than him, not of the same class. The child she bore him was taken away and left under a rock to be discovered, raised and educated by a chieftain. Another translation of the word Ailbe is 'alive under a stone'.

Thus one of the most ancient motifs since man became literate attached itself to this small, innocuous place – the belief that great people have unconventional birth. It happened to Moses, it happened to Christ, it ran rife among the gods. By it, nations created a figurehead or leader or deity, whose associations and circumstances, from the very beginning, had an out-of-the-ordinary quality, a divine aura sustaining both worshippers and worshipped.

Sub-legends usually followed. In Ailbe's case he became a slave of the Britons, among whom he acquired Christianity. He travelled as far as Rome, where he received holy orders, preached the whole way back and landed in Belfast. He then evangelized his way down Ireland and finally met Patrick, who made him a bishop on condition that – ingenious hierarchical thought – Ailbe could perform no miracles without Patrick's permission. He established his monastery at Emly in the second half of the fifth century and built a holy centre there, renowned for learning, missionary work and the warm welcome it gave to wandering priests.

In such establishments the physical edifice of the church dominated, a rectangular building of strong planks, where possible of local oak, otherwise of wattle daubed together with mixed mud. The cells of the monks, made of wicker and thatch, clustered around the church, the size of which remained remarkably small; even when the community expanded they built other churches according to the demand, rather than always enlarging the existing one. Two other buildings had importance, the refectory and the guest house, and in the case of the larger and more important monasteries a school completed the compound, which was the nearest the pre-Viking Irish ever came to having towns.

Nothing of Ailbe's time remains to be seen in Emly, though; only the name survives, enshrined in a Pugin-Gothic Victorian church which sits on the hill, visible for miles around, typical of the nineteenth-century statement of Irish rural Catholic power. The original monastery, developed from the flimsier wattle-and-daub buildings, suffered heavily from Vikings in the ninth century, and even though it flourished for many centuries afterwards, the friends of Henry VIII finally finished it off.

No traces remain either of the influence this little village had, or the importance of Ailbe, but if a great early medieval document such as *The Annals of Innisfallen* had truly been written here it needed the support of a deep background in learning, thought and intellectual stability. Even now, the countryside displays how it must have been able to maintain an important monastery. Such good earth on either side of the road, tilled land, with beef cattle, and large old trees, and houses in excellent repair; the prosperity of the farmers has kept this countryside stable for a couple of thousand years.

Ten miles further east the town of Tipperary, where I went to school, has the typical long main street of many Irish and Scottish towns, though in this case several other streets radiate off to the left up the hill, and to the right down the hill, towards the foothills of the mountains. Revolutions flared here; land war leaders came in from the countryside, debated the intellectual principles of democracy and plannned the practical, often brutal, strikes against landlordism. In the town itself the workers formed one of the very early soviets and raised the red flag over the gasworks, while a creamery in the outlying countryside joined in with the slogan, 'Knocklong Soviet Creamery – We Make Butter, Not Profits.'

The road east, past the graveyard where my father and sister are buried, climbs a hill to further feasts – a wide plain with one, two, three, castles in the distance: Grantstown, Thomastown and the fabulous Rock of Cashel. This castle and church stand on top of a limestone crag and still command the countryside; the modern town only stands and waits. An important place, Cashel of the Kings, a rallying point for the eyes and the hearts of the people of these plains, a place of inspiration and romance. From the Rock

'The magic that takes you far, far out, of this time and this world',
wrote Shaw – Skellig Michael and the small Skellig, eight miles
out in the Atlantic, seen from the coast of Kerry.

Macgillicuddy's Reeks, Ireland's highest mountains. According to folklore, the Skelligs originally formed two further peaks of this range, which dominates the south-east of County Kerry.

Aerial view of the beehive huts constructed by the community of fisher monks on Skellig Michael (above), and (below) Gallarus Oratory in County Kerry, built on the same principle and in the same spiritual tradition as the huts of Skellig Michael.

Lion, representing St Mark the Evangelist, from one of the earliest Irish manuscripts, the seventh/eighth-century *Book of Durrow*.

One of Irish art's earliest representations of the Crucifixion, this hammered gilt bronze plaque from the late seventh or early eighth century is believed to have decorated the cover of a religious book.

Seventh-century carved whalebone casket from Northumbria,
showing Frankish influences. Pagan and Christian traditions are
wedded: on the left is the Germanic mythological figure Wieland
the Smith; on the right the Magi march under a star.

The sands of Iona (above) owe their famous whiteness to deposits
of calcium carbonate from the sea-bed borne in shoals
across from the Hebrides.
'Cut off on the landward side by very deep water, and facing on
the other side the limitless ocean', as Bede described it, Lindisfarne
(below) lies a mile and a half off the shore of Northumbria.

King David playing the harp, from the eighth-century *Psalter of St Augustine*.

of Cashel, the spectacular view alerted the kings of Munster. In the centre of the horizon to the north sits the Devil's Bit mountain, a peak with a chunk taken out. Patrick chased Lucifer down these fields, and when the fleeing demon found a mountain in his way he took a bite and spat it out at Cashel.

In the entrance hall museum on this Rock they display a Hallstatt sword. The definition means not that it comes from that little village in the Austrian Alps, but – regardless of where it was manufactured – from the early period of Celtic culture, anywhere from 750 BC to·500 BC, descended from, or belonging to, a pattern of metalworking from eastern mainland Europe. (The man who discovered this sword in County Tipperary took it around in the boot of his car for a while, showing it to friends and neighbours, before sending it to the experts.) Another twenty or thirty miles to the north, gorgets turned up in the earth – semicircular configured neckbands, rich personal ornaments. Unique around here, and thought to have German origins, they were made of gold, hallmarks of wealth and comfort. Maybe the sword was owned by a farmer, for protection; equally likely, it belonged to a warrior. The gorgets, though, tell a clearer, firmer story.

The people of these parts who owned such goods had a society and economy of some depth, a long prehistory of cultivation, fought for and protected by the warrior class. By the time of Christ they knew their land well, had tamed it, worked it, legislated for it, through a thousand, perhaps fifteen hundred years. Their lives moved slowly; like many of their countrymen around Ireland, they had traded usefully with Europe. Even passing through, you can feel their depth still. Today, they continue to own comfortable farms and benefit from the wealth of their produce and the bonus of all the food they might need. The continental connection persists; many of these homes grew wealthy through European Community grants.

In the shadow of the Rock, I had no difficulty whatsoever imagining a monk walking through these fields thirteen centuries ago. His welcome was assured: 'respect for the cloth' prevails here, and for learning, and for the endeavours of holy pilgrims. Parish excursions leave for Knock, the Marian shrine in the west of Ireland, and flights are chartered to Lourdes.

Of all the territories through which he might pass, this place offered as much safety as the monk might meet; here the Dark Ages shone brightly enough. In any case he came from the same stock, with the same social and cultural and religious references. Life around here has changed little – the same landscape, farmed by the descendants of the same people that met Patrick, took in his word and followed his followers.

They spoke Gaelic, an Indo-European language, reshaped by time and nomads from the European Celtic – I learned it at school. They had been trained to be practical countryside dwellers, hewers of wood and drawers

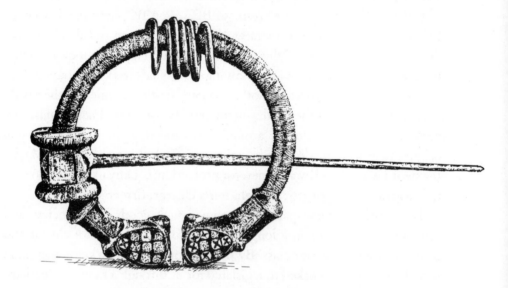

Enamelled bronze brooch from County Offaly.

of water, and to spend hour after hour upon their knees praying to God. This area supplied the many monasteries of the county with monks; in the local towns, the boys' schools enjoyed a reputation envied all across Munster for providing vocations to the priesthood.

So I stayed a night in Cashel of the Kings, a small town with a tiny population. It still prides itself on the royal antecedents, and the wide main street offers glimpses of the stunning Rock and the enchanted limestone complex on top of it. From any angle, in any light, at sunset or at dawn, or floodlit on a rainy night, it fulfils every visual and imaginative impression of the fairytale Celtic castle, a place of wishes and princes. Magic flutters around the place, in pre-Christian whispers. High on the wall squats a rowdy-faced sheelagh-na-gig, a randy fertility symbol. Put your arms around the trunk of the cross in the courtyard and you will be free of toothache forever. Then, the Christian powers: on certain solstices the angle of the architrave on Cormac's Chapel corresponds with the direction of the sun's rays. When Patrick arrived here, Natfraich, the King of Munster, according to one account, 'congratulated him'. On what? On sticking his crozier through the uncomplaining foot of Aengus, Natfraich's son, during the baptism ceremony until 'the blood flowed down the side of the rock'?

Looking back, from a few miles along the Dublin road, the Rock seemed to grow in enchantment through the morning showers and sunshine, a fortress where, typically, the secular and the sacred lived side by side. Twenty years ago the courtyard facing north had been dominated by a great Celtic cross, which commemorated a local nineteenth-century landlord, ' a bad pill' named Scully. When a storm broke the cross in two the people said, 'He had it coming to him.' Time will always have a very slow march here.

This main road joins the Republic's two largest cities, Dublin and Cork. More alluring signposts: Horse and Jockey, Boherlahan (meaning 'the wide road') and eventually my next ancient stage, Kildare; Cill Dara, 'the church of the oak tree'. I left Cashel early, aiming to reach Kildare mid-morning, on an empty road save for occasional tractors, some going to the peat bog at Littleton.

I stopped briefly in Durrow, again derived from the Gaelic/Celtic word for oak tree – *dara*. Here, before he left Ireland – amid political difficulty – for Iona, Columba was once believed to have written *The Book of Durrow*. This relatively small, very beautiful, illuminated manuscript of the Gospels, now in the care of Trinity College, Dublin, lights up the second half of the seventh century. The style of the decorated script belongs to the late mainstream of Celtic civilization. The craftsmen who pioneered western European ornamentation of this standard worked in the same tradition of whorls, leaf patterns, tendrils, spirals and interlacing now synonymous with the words 'Celtic Art'. They dropped capitals and designed introductions to each chapter by creating entire pages of illumination, carpeting the vellum with multitudinous patterns of the greatest intricacy.

The Book of Durrow has all the power not only of a single major work of art but of an entire movement, a school of endeavour. Although the volume was conceived as an act of worship, it has had secular reverberations far beyond that. The capacity for the fantastic would do a science fiction illustrator proud, and the presence of animals and beasts in the interiors of the drawings takes it and its themes out of the devotional arena and creates an earthiness and a menace which question the roots of the religion to which it subscribes.

Eagle illumination from *The Book of Durrow*.

Sadly for local pride, the essence and fame of Durrow was conceived elsewhere. It was kept in the monastery here, perhaps in memory of Columba, but its neatness of hand, elegance of accomplishment and evidence of the spread of influences – Anglo-Saxon and Coptic – all mark it down as Northumbrian in authorship.

Brigid of Kildare bids fair to be the most powerful female icon figure in western Europe. Boadicea, the warrior queen, rebelled because she had been unjustly treated. Queen Mab of the fairies may never have existed, or, if she did, had to share an identity with Queen Maeve of Connaught, the warlady of the mythologies. Brigid towered over them all, right alongside Patrick in Irish sainthood. Her name and some of her magic efficacy descended from the pagan goddess of many hues and places and benefactions, known in France and Britain – Brighid, or Bride, or Brigantia. The gift of woman's fertility had so much actual and emblematic importance that followers became eager to praise it further with other marvellous attributions.

She cured ailments of the eye and the head and the limbs. She hung her clothes to dry on the rays of the sun. She had two sisters of the same name and this fecund trinity was born of the Daghda, the greatest god in Celtic mythology, who had an insatiable appetite for both porridge and sexual intercourse (though in what order the myths never quite specified).

Brigid the saint founded a convent in Kildare by a stratagem. When she approached a local landowner for a gift of land to build a monastery, he told her contemptuously that she could have as many acres as her cloak would cover. Brigid laid her cloak on the ground, and it spread and spread. She gained enough land to found a famous establishment which she and her nuns shared with the monks of a nearby monastery – to whom they could only speak through an oaken screen. It did not prevent Brigid, they say, from proposing to Patrick who, sworn to celibacy, turned her down and also prevented women from ever proposing to men again, except once in four years, on the leap-year day of February.

The magic persisted. Brigid's convent of twenty nuns had among their tasks the guardianship of a perpetual fire, surrounded by a ring of shrubs, entry through which was absolutely forbidden to any man. Furthermore, Brigid herself had been born at sunrise on 1 February, one of the four great feasts in the pagan Celtic calendar, when the lambs drew milk from the ewes.

The monastery of Kildare, vanished now, stood at the spot where she had once spread her cloak. The graveyard and the church were completely deserted on that rainy morning when I visited them. A notice advertising the perpetual appeal for the restoration of the buildings had begun to yellow in the rain; Brigid is becoming more remote, supplanted by recent saints. The town outside stands at a crossroads of rich farms where the great horses of the flat racing world have been bred and trained for centuries; the grass, grown on strata of limestone, builds calcium and strong bones. On the edge of the town, at the National Stud, the mares are falsely induced into heat by a conducive atmosphere of artificial light and environment – so the fecundity of the goddess Brigid has an appealing modern application.

I drove north through the Curragh of Kildare. Ptolemy called Dublin Portus Eblanorum. The old name for the area was Eblana; the Vikings developed the site a long time afterwards. In the seventh century the entire area around the city was regarded as dangerous land; today the acres of poverty-stricken urban developments bleed with social pain – drugs and homelessness rather than wild boar or wolves. The only reason a Christian pilgrim of the seventh century would have had for visiting Dublin was to see for himself the place where Patrick is said to have landed and to have founded a church, now St Patrick's Cathedral, by a well which sprang up when he stabbed the ground with his crozier while seeking water to baptize his new converts.

Patrick's actual landing place has been disputed. One ancient source says he landed at Drogheda, a port some thirty miles north of Dublin; others argue for Wicklow, in the opposite direction; while a third says he landed in Dublin itself. The only benefit to be gained from a visit to Dublin in pursuit of a Dark Ages wanderer is that the museum illuminates the secular life of the period.

Ireland had a small population in a wooded country – deep, dense forests, some less impenetrable woodland and open birchwood; the large inland seas of Kildare, thirty miles to the south-west, had only recently (geologically speaking) dried up. The peasant society, self-governing by simple election, had recognizable strata and divisions based on skills, learning, warrior prowess and priesthood. The judges had laws to use, the poets had metrical structures, the families had alliances. When Patrick travelled through Ireland the kingship system prevailed, and the families with riches had slaves and glory. Two hundred years later, any holy pilgrim received a welcome from the same great families in their palaces.

Stature revealed itself by the usual European systems – forms of dress, ornamentation, quality of personal possession. The noblemen and women wore tunics of linen covered by outer cloaks of wool, many of them multi-coloured, with much gold and jewelled ornamentation. The more exalted the woman the more beautiful her costume, with exquisite brooches in leaf shapes; the men went into battle dressed for impressiveness, bearing shields with scalloped edges. Above all, land divided the classes: 'as much land as his eye could measure' defined a rich man; 'as much as his cloak could cover' befitted a poor one.

Around the central room of the huge thatched house extended cubicles, like bedrooms or ante-rooms, slept in by many members of the family on hides and animal skins. In lesser houses the sleepers took up positions by the walls, still within the light and heat of the fire, but not occupying the central eating and living place. Outside, in a large yard, domestic animals fed and slept, behind wooden fortifications reinforcing outer earthen ramparts. No Roman occupation had taken place, so no stone ruins could be cannibalized for building houses. Class related largely to agriculture; royalty and aristocrats came from those who farmed the largest ranches. Alongside them the priest, the monk, the abbot filled the role of honour always allotted in terms of intellectual prowess and spiritual integrity, even though the days of the Druids had long gone. Beneath this top stratum of society, smaller farmers, tenants and freemen gave to a king, a chieftain or an abbot their tribute in food or produce, such as wool, leather or precious metals. They ate meat, largely pork, some smoked or boiled fish, a little bread loosely and soggily baked with rough oats, and they drank wheaten beer sweetened with honey.

Other places further along had more relevance to my traveller. I took the Navan road out of Dublin to County Meath, wide, rich and royal, with the Hill of Tara still a touchstone for romantic legend and myth. Tara rises above the plain of the Boyne valley, and up to the eighth century had a powerful part to play in the national body and mind. Five provinces shared Ireland – Munster to the south, Leinster to the east, Ulster to the north, Connaught to the west and Tara, the governing province. Here the High Kings of Ireland were chosen on the most renowned, if not quite the most archaeologically valuable, Celtic hillfort.

The name Tara means a wide vista – the first line of defence consists in seeing the enemy approach. The excavations here revealed a passage grave dated to before 2000 BC, in which had been buried a boy wearing beads of Egyptian influence. At Tara the new king mated with the earth; on this mound a pair of stones parted to let the chariot of the rightful king drive through, and a stone phallus, still standing – Lia Fail, the Stone of Destiny

– screamed when touched by the man who would be king. Almost every facet of mythology and early history seems to have been represented at Tara – taboos, bonds, law enactment, the divine right of kings, heroic endeavour, curses, ritual, feasts, births and burials. Now the place has been graced with an unfortunate statue of Patrick which weather and vandals have damaged – but not nearly enough.

I followed the course of the Boyne from Tara. This valley has some of the most accessible antiquity in the world. Knowledge of the passage grave at Tara offered only an advertisement of what was to come. The Boyne, which rises in Carbury in County Kildare, several miles away, never becomes a broad or powerful river, never expands into no more than a wide and reasonably placid stream. People who live on the banks speak of the fact that by day the waters flow dark and at night they gleam brightly.

Beneath the ground, though, the Boyne valley exercises the greatest power. At the passage graves of Knowth, Dowth and Newgrange the deep, long corridors end at burial chambers. In the archaeological drawings, each tomb appears like an exaggerated version of the medical symbol for the female – a long, skinny neck culminating in a small cross.

Newgrange, the largest of them, whose name some have tried to translate as 'the cave of the sun', is reached by a series of small side roads, country lanes, past the entrances to quiet farms. The exterior resembles some enormous grass-covered amphitheatre, high and white, with a dome of grass and earth. The reconstruction returned Newgrange to the days of glory – long before the Pyramids or Stonehenge. Ancient bones rested in this place, the most holy ground of pagan Ireland, and any early Christian coming upon Newgrange had cause to shudder and pray to his new god.

At the entrance stands a large stone embossed with whorls which mirror the river looping through the trees down at the bottom of the hill. The passage, flanked by tall boulders etched with more designs, geometric, almost mechanical or astral, draws the soul far into the tomb to the stone dish where the burnt bones of the dead resided. Directly over the entrance to the tomb a slot appears in the roof, which the guide described as 'the light-box'. Newgrange disappeared for years under the hill, as the grass overgrew it and the earth piled up; eventually a seventeenth-century antiquarian rediscovered the great tomb and later excavations revealed this light-box. In such investigations archaeology and mathematical science can have common purpose, and the possibilities of Newgrange emerged. The light-box had a specific, ritual function.

On a clear morning of the winter solstice – frost makes ideal weather – the rising sun, as it comes over the far hill, filters slowly at first into this light-box, fingering its young eastern light up along the passage of the grave, turning the stones to light gold. When fully risen, the sun floods the stone dish deep in the heart of the chamber, as if bathing the dead with the only warmth available in winter. Then the light slips away again back down the passage and out into the fields, as the sun climbs higher into the winter morning sky.

❖

After Newgrange, I turned away from the main Dublin–Belfast road to look for the abbeys of Mellifont and Monasterboice. Unlike a wandering scholar I could have no shelter among them unless I bedded down among the stone ruins and ragwort at Monasterboice.

If I had been a wandering monk arriving at a monastery like these in 687 the monks would have welcomed me with open arms and questioned me for any political or ecclesiastical or monastic gossip. In a strict regime they had a benign and familial atmosphere. They spoke Gaelic, and they also had Latin; the extensive contact with the continent of Europe received boosts from visiting monks or returning missionaries, and this constant fertilization helped the Irish monasteries to establish their unique character. Lecturers at Trinity College, Dublin in the early part of this century made these observations:

Egypt furnished the original type and imparted the original tone. The Irish schools then developed themselves in accordance with their own genius. They had one pre-eminent quality, distinguishing them … they pursued learning for its own sake. They did not require to be bribed by prizes and scholarships. They conceived and rightly conceived that learning was its own reward. The schools had moderate landed endowments, and their teaching was apparently free to all, or at any rate, imparted at a very low charge. Bede tells us that Irish professors were in the habit of receiving English pupils, educating, feeding, and supplying them with books without making any charge at all …. They lived under very simple conditions of society. They had no solid halls or buildings; a few wattled huts constituted their college. They lived an *al fresco* life. They taught and studied in the open air ... yet they had an organised system. They usually had a chief or senior lecturer. They had professors of law, of poetry, of history and other branches of education. They had an *oeconomus*, or steward, who managed the temporal affairs of the institution. They had special schools, too, some of which lasted till modern times. The union of law and history ... was not unknown there ....

I left Mellifont and headed across country, bypassing the town of Dundalk, and turning my face to the plains of glory. These small fields and hills of scrub and gorse suggest no grandeur, bear no trace of the huge and epic exploits that gave a people an entire prehistory, yet here the cycles of legend were spun.

The names give some clue – Ardee, the ford of Ferdia, boyhood friend and eventually mortal enemy of the great Cuchulainn. Who was the son of Lugh of the Long Arm, father and son each a Celtic Apollo. Who slew hundreds and thousands in bloody combat and turned the rivers of these plains red with blood. Who resisted the temptations and blandishments of witches and goddesses and shape shifters and lovers and Druids. Who campaigned and rampaged through aeons of fireside histories, and who created icons for rebels and children.

From here to Armagh, the fields are crammed with such ancient mysteries and memories. The three daughters of a wizard conjured the sounds of battle and the sights of phantom armies to make it seem as if the valley was afire with battle and therefore lure Cuchulainn forth. Cuchulainn's battle ardour stirred; in battle ardour his body gyrated within his skin, each hair on his head sprang out into a spark of flame and a burning aura surrounded his head. Torn with wounds and his life blood ebbing away, he lashed himself to a pillar so that he might stay upright and not fall before his enemies, and they, so fearful of his reputation, kept their distance and only knew he had died when a black bird, the raven goddess of death, came and perched upon the hero's shoulder.

I travelled on through Cuchulainn's warfields, north through Ravensdale and Faughart, where St Brigid is supposed to have been born, where the weathering of various stones has produced configurations that to this day are credited with having descended straight from the saint. Into the head stone, hollowed by rain and geological change, you put your head if you suffer from headaches. An eye stone collects rainwater in which you bathe your ailing eyes. Kneel in the knee stone for anguished joints. Ahead, over the hill by a cemetery, the Gap of the North opens out, and I am struck by how relevant the symbolism of mythology remains.

The cycles relating to Cuchulainn are full of tales of Ulster's sickness, Ulster's wasting, Ulster's capitulation to the forces which threatened its province. When called upon to defend themselves the Ulstermen refused, because for several days at a time they lay under a curse which made them

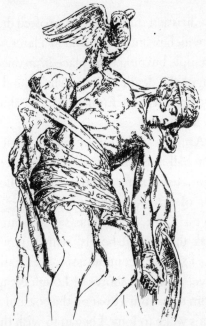

The death throes of Cuchulainn: statue in the General Post Office, Dublin.

more feeble than a woman giving birth. Three times in one morning I was stopped on the road by men with guns and uniforms. One patrol came from an army regiment, while the two other platoons brought me back to the legends. These, from the Ulster Defence Regiment, stopped me, with minimum civility, on a small road – ironic twist – near Armagh, and the road led me to the fort of Emhain Macha, without doubt still famous in the seventh century, perhaps still populated then, and still echoing with the stories which transferred across from the pagan to the Christian tradition.

This fortress, named for a goddess who could outrun a chariot, had almost as much power and importance as Tara, and here a great temple was built, with 'a rooftree a hundred feet high', a temple large enough 'to hold a thousand people'. The labour to build this temple lasted surely for several years and within these earthen ramparts – still there, still high and grassy – they erected hollow wooden walls which they filled with stones. Then one day, for no traceable reason, they burnt the temple to the ground. Nobody knows why; it may have been a sacrifice to the gods, it may have been an economic decision, but having built the equivalent of a great cathedral they razed it.

At this point the Christian tradition, as it so often did, commandeered the legend and the fact which prompted it, and in a later, suitably created myth suggested that the temple burning took place in an unconscious, synchronistic commemoration of the death of Jesus Christ, and that on the day now called Good Friday the earth of Emhain Macha shuddered and the king murmured, 'A god has died.'

Apple country, Armagh, where they play a curious game. It involves throwing a cast-iron ball along the road, judging nicely the camber of the tarmacadam to negotiate corners, and the person who covers a set distance in the least number of throws is the winner. They play the same game further south in west Cork, and some say it comes from the time of Cuchulainn; in Cork they call it bowls, which they pronounce 'bowels'; here, with even less fortunate connotations, they call it 'bullets'.

I intended to travel along the shores of Lough Neagh, home of Ireland's first settlers, and from there join a boat on the coast of Antrim which would take me in Columba's wake to Iona. I began to wish that the basalt stepping stones of the Giant's Causeway, specially provided for Finn McCool to walk across the sea, stretched north to the islands rather than east to mainland Scotland. I discovered why even a giant like Finn needed a causeway: boatman after boatman found the Atlantic too mighty. The journey takes more than a ferryman's wage and skill; these waters run high and deep.

I arranged to join Andy Seaton at the harbourmaster's office in Portrush and from his boat, the *Carole E*, I would clamber on to thàt same 'sloping westerly beach' kissed by Columba and his monks on 12 May 563. Andy, on the telephone, said the wind had moved to the north and the seas were running very high. No chance? No. If we were to try – how many more days should I wait? Impossible to say – this was Tuesday – it could be the weekend. And no chance of trying to catch the tide tomorrow just after noon? No.

I had wanted to retrace Columba's journey to the footstep, though that would have involved leaving his city of Derry (other sources say he left from Howth, the great hill that lies snouting like a pig across Dublin Bay), and furthermore I should have been bringing with me an uncle, two cousins and the son of a king in a party of twelve.

On some island I long to be,
a rocky promontory, looking on
the coiling surface of the sea.

To see the waves, crest on crest
of the great shining ocean, composing
a hymn to the creator, without rest.

To see without sadness the strand
lined with bright shells, and birds
lamenting overhead, a lonely sound.

To hear the whisper of small waves
against the rocks, that endless sea-
sound, like keening over graves.

COLUMBA
trans. John Montague

CHAPTER TWO

THE WHISPER OF SMALL WAVES

THEY SET FORTH in a giant coracle made of cattle hides and willow basketwork. Under a cloud too. Columba is believed to have accepted an enforced exile after some political, legal and military business not compatible with the holy calling of a monk. Copyright law entered the issue, with accusations of copying a book, and a famous Irish judgement: 'To every cow her calf and to every book its copy'.

Columba on his stated mission to travel into exile for Christ – *pro Christo peregrinari volens* – had not intended Iona as his destination. He imposed upon himself a condition, that he could only disembark in a place from whose highest point he could never again see Ireland. First of all he stopped at Dunadd, the great fort in Argyll, where the Irish kings of Dalriada ruled the west of Scotland. Next he found that the high points of Jura and the islands of Islay, Oronsay and Colonsay still yielded glimpses of distant Ireland, so he settled for Iona, a small flitter on the edge of the west Highlands, a blip on the map of this ravishing archipelago.

I had no choice but to get there by long and mundane means, by ferry from Oban to Mull, then by road to Fionnphort, 'the white bay', for another ferry crossing across the short sound to Iona, over to this stub of land, a liturgical powerbase which had fair claims to being called the Rome of the North.

> On some island I long to be,
> a rocky promontory, looking on
> the coiling surface of the sea.
>
> To see the waves, crest on crest
> of the great shining ocean, composing
> a hymn to the creator, without rest.
>
> To see without sadness the strand
> lined with bright shells, and birds
> lamenting overhead, a lonely sound.
>
> To hear the whisper of small waves
> against the rocks, that endless sea-
> sound, like keening over graves.

Columba's poem confirms his desire for exile.

They call the little bay where he landed the Port of the Coracles, a small sloping beach divided in two by an outcrop of rock that reaches out some thirty feet into the sea. To edge into this otherwise very safe landing place the boat would have had to negotiate several stiff bunches of rock further out, and ease itself on to the sloping shingle – although the word 'shingle' does small service to this deep tray of stones of all colours and smoothnesses. A million stones lie here, forty million years old, and they twinkle with red and silver, and have jewelled names too, like mica and marble and quartz and gneiss and augite and silica and schist and tremolite and trachite and glittering crystal and yellow epidote and green hornblende and feldspar the colour of bleeding rouge. Uncomfortable underfoot, though, and as I turned my back to this clean and historic water to my right I saw the Hill of the Back of Ireland, where Columba at last assured himself that he could no longer see the land of his birth.

He did flex a little; a dozen years after his establishment on Iona he returned to Ireland for a conference of some political and ecclesiastical importance, and in order that he could never be accused of breaking his vows he remained blindfolded for the year of the conference's duration, with high clods of turf from Iona bound to the soles of his feet. H'm.

It is true, though, that from the Hill of the Back of Ireland you cannot see the Irish coast from which I had hoped to sail. You can see other coasts and flat-topped outcrop islands and even a needle of lighthouse in the blue distance. My own monk must also have set forth across Iona to find the monastery. (If you are obliged to come by the ferry route I have already described you cannot miss the monastery, but that is another matter.)

From the rock where Columba could not see Ireland a sheep had fallen and died; a roughish walk only if your expectations are of an easy and green place, and on the crest of another hill a long narrow loch has pipes leading from it and spares lying about the ground – the loch feeds the freshwater needs of the village. Now a view opened to the north and more islands and coasts of wonder, little Atlantises, appeared far away. Which one is Ulva, and where is Staffa, where Mendelssohn was inspired to write *Fingal's Cave*? White sands fringe the green open common of Iona. The satellite photographs have apparently shown deposits of calcium carbonate, brilliant white moving across the sea like great white shoals and coming to rest on the beaches of the Western Isles.

Open ground again; tufted and comfortable after the rocky path descending from the loch. I opted for the farthest end to get to the highest point of the island, a rocky peaklet from which, according to the map, I would be able to see the entire place. I kept the sea on my left hand and walked across the broad turf, up into heights along the first of many misleading paths. They did seem as if they had been travelled daily by humans, these wide and sensible paths between the rocks, but time after time they petered out on tops of crags leaving only a sheer drop to a beach or rocky inlet 150 feet below. Then I realized that sheep care nothing for scenery, and sweet grasses can be found right up to the edges of the cliffs.

I turned insland and found myself in a small wild valley, not a human trace, nor an animal's, only a deep and slightly treacherous marshland. A struggling walk this country, not easy; to make my way up towards the high point I had to work hard. *En route* the square tower of the abbey building appeared.

The monastery proved useless to me; late medieval, and therefore irritating. Traces of Columba exist, though; nearby earthen ramparts, subjected to detailed excavation, located the site of the monastery more precisely – in the shelter of Iona's highest peak, the Dun I, and a little to the west of the existing buildings but underlapping them. In the graveyard a descent of kings is buried – Irish, Scottish, Scandinavian, before, contemporary with, and after Columba, including (again maddeningly outside my brief) Macbeth.

In the interrogation of Columban Iona two sources, archaeology and the biography of the saint, describe the settlement as it existed when Columba founded it and as it must have stayed, more or less, for the next two hundred years. He had precise dates: he arrived on the feast of Pentecost – how full of coincidences hagiography can be, since Columba means 'dove' and, according to some sources, Iona means 'dove' in Hebrew – and he died on 6 June 597, aged seventy-seven.

The monastery consisted of a large central cell, Columba's own, on higher ground and a little away from the others, in which he slept on a stone slab using a piece of rectangular granite for a pillow. Around this building, each monk had his own cell. They gathered during the day and night for community work and prayer in the monastery buildings, which included a church whose oak beams were sailed across from the mainland of Argyll or the isle of Mull half a mile away. By the fireplace in the refectory sat a stone vessel in which the feet of arriving pilgrims were washed, according to the rules of hospitality which transcended all other disciplines on the island.

Columba had his own writing place and the monastery had a *scriptorium; The Book of Kells*, early western Christianity's most elaborate ancient manuscript, is believed to have been created on Iona, and taken to Ireland to escape the ravages of marauders.

Barns, sheds and a refectory completed the large settlement which, at the highest point of Columba's reign, held 150 monks. Whispers of early lives came to light during excavations – a piece of red slipware from North Africa, a midden containing the bones of animals, domestic refuse, clay moulds for making glass beads, a tiny bell, traces of a kiln for drying corn – and they seem to corroborate, one way and another the biographical details included by a later abbot, Adamnan, who wrote *Vita Sancti Columbae*.

Iona held a clearly defined community, with known and agreed tasks, divided among seniors or elders, a middle stratum of workers and the juniors, novices and learner monks. Each Wednesday and Friday they fasted, each Saturday they rested, and each Saturday night and all day on Sunday they knelt or walked in prayer. Adamnan portrayed these hardworking men wearing white cowled tunics, leather sandals and a tonsure. No trace of them here now; the abbey, handed on by a series of trusts and gifts, is maintained in Christian fellowship, non-denominational, and the friendly hotel filled up with singing Christians from the north of England.

One of the symbols of the Evangelists from *The Book of Kells*.

Previous travellers have referred to the peace of Iona. Undeniably, it has a soothing, eye-bathing tranquillity. Equally unquestionably, the propaganda of Christianity attributed this quality to Columba and the sanctity of his settlement. But it may have occurred the other way round – Columba and his landing party may have found the combination of colours in the sea and on the beaches, and the undulating green ground, conducive to worship.

They arrived in May, remember, the time of the year when Iona may possibly look its most beautiful. Their first view, to the west, showed no other great or threatening lands, and the openness of the green plain they saw ahead of them still – deceptively – suggests fertility. The island has no harshness, at least nothing alarming, and even where the cliffs do have threatening faces they give way to exquisite sands. Peace, yes, from nature – therefore, in their terms, from God. Iona provided the perfect opportunity to offer prayer and sacrifice while staying in touch with a tangible slice of the natural world so beloved of Irish monks.

Columba evangelized forth from here, to the islands and the Highlands, to the Picts and the other peoples of Scotland. On his way to their souls he often performed miracles for their bodies. He cured a wife of her loveless distaste for her husband; he fought off the ancestors of the Loch Ness monster; he calmed unfavourable winds; he healed a mysterious illness in a wizard – by making him drink water in which he placed a pebble he had blessed; and he created a firm and influential input into the politics of Scotland and Ireland. Columba walked the corridors of power and became a grey eminence in the affairs of the people who were called Scotii, who came from Ireland and gave their name to Scotland.

The ferry from Iona to Fionnphort on Mull only takes a few minutes and the Christians, some of them, stood on deck praying with each other. Mull has stunning views. The road, single-tracked to test the coach drivers, sweeps by long lochs with red columns of mountain in the near distance. From Craignure the larger ferry sails to Oban several times a day, and from the top deck the views open down along long narrow sea lanes to isles, gorse-lit fjords and Sir Walter Scott castles on crags. Oban feels like a Norse town, overlooked by an eyeless, unfinished colosseum, a charitable man's folly, started by him to keep unemployed masons in work. When my monk crossed from Mull, Oban had long been in existence, a large Bronze Age settlement of hunters and fishermen who left ancient spoor in the caves nearby.

The road to Lochgilphead turned out to be one of the most beautiful roads I have ever travelled. I hope my monk saw the same views: he would have chanted aloud psalms to the glory of his God. From time to time, breaks in the trees and in the crags revealed small harbours with boats and cottages; mountains in the distance, Jura, and long waters. Off the narrow roads, lanes and byways invited and intrigued. It would have been quite possible never to reach the end of this journey. I had to make one essential stop, though, in the valley of the small River Add. I survived the temptation of some standing stones in a field to the right, and beyond Kilmichael, at the end of a long straight dusty lane, I climbed Dunadd.

It rises out of marshy land on a sudden rocky height, and the fortifications can still be seen in ascending interfacing walls, making the place impregnable. The entrance is gained through a short narrow pathway. A little defile hemmed in by stones, it could still be defended by one man. Winding around another old wall I reached a small open plateau and then, further up, through a larger 'gateway' of rock, the pathway bends to the right and eventually to the summit.

Shades of Cashel and Tara and Armagh: again I stood on a place which commanded great views of the countryside all around – a boy and a dog could be seen with clarity by the watchman. On the ground a small stone held rainwater in it, used in the consecration of kings here. Dunadd, one of the four Dalriada capital forts, had a powerful significance in the Irish government of early Scotland. Nearby, a footprint in the rock selected the king; if the foot fitted, the king had stepped into the royal shoes. On the rock beside the footprint careful tracing reveals a boar etched in stone, a Pictish symbol, they say, though the boar has rampaged across at least one Celtic legend – in the Fenian cycle, where Diarmuid, who has stolen Finn McCool's lover, Grainne, is gored to eventual death by a wild boar. Tremendous hospitality was available here too, especially for somebody bringing a letter – or some other identifying means of introduction – from the Abbot of Iona.

A sudden depression came in, not from the sea or the sky, but from the spirit. Perhaps those investigators of the paranormal have a point, that the smell of ancient bloodshed hangs in the air to haunt future generations. Dunadd must have seen a share of violence and intrigue. I have heard tales of people who wandered unwittingly on to old battlefields, such as bloody Culloden, and were overcome with deep melancholy and suicidal depressions, and who then returned to their hosts in bemused and sad frame of mind, and were not surprised at all to find that they had been traversing bloodstained ground. My mood changed the moment I climbed this rock. 'Be alone in a separate place near a chief city', said the Rule of Columba, 'if thy conscience is not prepared to be in common with the crowd.'

I was tempted to linger, to wander out to the islands and track down all the saints who lived out there in caves. I could have gone, for instance, to Holy Island, by Lochranza and Brodick on Arran, to the cave of Maol Iosa, St Maolaise, 'the chosen son of Jesus', one of Columba's disciples whose marks are still on the wall there. Instead, I headed for a point much farther south.

Rain hammered across Galloway, hard rain, the road hopped with it. Not much stands between these strong-housed farms and the sea; the wind prevails from the west. Again the landscape has not changed; no geological upheavals, no landslips or earthquakes. Centuries of rain and wind have caused small weathering, but not enough to change the horizon since the Dark Ages. The town of Whithorn, small, long and grey, which begins on a hill with a signpost to St Ninian's Cave and ends at the Black Hawk inn, scarcely possesses a single side street.

To the west of Whithorn, by the farms of Physgill in the area called Glasserton, a signpost advertises the car park for St Ninian's Cave. Callers at the end of this long winding private road are invited to place tenpence in the box, which in itself exhibits a Scottish cliché: the collection box for these tenpences consists of a huge safe, of the type usually found in old banks, some four feet high and two feet thick. A path leads through a private wood, down by a burn which develops a spate – headlong it pours, through birches and old beeches. The path breaks out into open ground after a short walk, and then falls down with the stream to the sea and ends in a small cove. In the cliffside a small cave opens, very high but not deep. As much as any place in Galilee, as much as any Aramaic retreat, as much as any closed and festered haunt of a Stylite, this shore represents the eastern tradition of the holy man who withdrew from society to fast, to pray, to mortify the body and invigorate the soul.

The waves ran high, leaving giant-sized saliva along the steep edges of the sloping shingle. On my left, at the entrance to the cave, some pilgrims had left a series of small crosses, sticks tied with thread or cord – on several different pilgrimages by the looks of them, since each cross seemed to have a distinctive personality. On the wall another series of crosses, very old, had been carved with care and emphasis, the simplest ones with T shapes on the extremities. Further in, through the steady trickle of water from the overhang, more pilgrim crosses lay on the ground, one tied with tinfoil, one made with wire and quite good wood, and many made of twigs tied with grasses. One had a note tied to it; no need to feel squeamish about prying into another person's votive hopes – the note, encased in clear plastic, had every intention of being read. 'To any pilgrim who reads this: Ninian the Great cured me I thank him and Almighty God.'

Immediate fascination: cured of what – the palsy, the dropsy, or other biblical ailment, or buboes from some strange Galloway plague? Or the effects of radiation – Galloway took an extra blast of Chernobyl's fallout, and the mutton remains unsafe. And 'To any pilgrim' assumed not just any but many pilgrims to Ninian's Cave. On the evidence of the little crosses, at least twenty people had worshipped or prayed here in the recent past. The view from the warm and sheltered interior of the cave gives only light and water: some divine architect, no doubt knowing of this place's potential as an anchorite retreat, had angled the mouth of the cave so that as little land as possible might be seen.

Freestanding crosses, taken from here for safety a century ago and now in the Whithorn museum, bear one exquisitely incised distinguishing pattern. This, the symbol of the Whithorn Trust which conducts the archaeological investigation of the ancient monastic site in the town, comes directly from the association with St Ninian. Called the marigold cross, it encases the arms of the simple T cross within a circle and compares with the shape of a flower. We are back again in attractive theological territory, where the old connection with nature still flourished and had not given away fully to the new religion.

The land undulates in tailored farms between here and Whithorn, and at the little bay which marks the isle of Whithorn, and with a ruined chapel named for, and probably descended from, an earlier building of St Ninian, a fishing trawler got ready to put out.

'In the year of our Lord 565,' wrote the Venerable Bede,

when Justin, the younger, the successor of Justinian, had the government of the Roman Empire, there came into Britain a famous priest and abbot, a monk by habit and life, whose name was Columba, to preach the word of God to the provinces of the northern Picts, who are separated from the southern parts by steep and rugged mountains; for the southern Picts, who dwell on this side of those mountains, had long before, it is reported, forsaken the errors of idolatry, and embraced the truth, by the preaching of Ninias, a most reverend bishop and holy man of the British nation.

Bede's statement has never needed much by way of gloss. This holy Welshman, Ninian, whose monastic training took place in Tours where French is said to be spoken at its most accentless perfect, built a monastery not of wattles or even oak, but of stone. (Whether he should have played down the Tours connection offers the possibility for some speculation. Martin of Tours, an unkempt little pleb, relinquished his commission in the Roman army and took up residence with a band of followers in the cliffs along the river at Marmoutier, whence he went forth to work miracles for the country folk and attack Roman shrines with a hatchet.)

In 1984 an archaeological dig began at Whithorn, and it intensified in 1986. The results proved enormously useful, both in terms of new knowledge and in confirmation of the history of the site as Scotland's earliest recorded Christian community. In the red shadow of the medieval priory they have assembled caravans and sheets of polythene, and in a dark building on the street outside, where the welcome is warm, students and archaeologists assemble the record from Ninian onwards.

The ground lies stripped open, cut in trenches. The archaeologists' minds refuse to be impressed by the sight of a skull, round and bone-white, peeping out of the cross-section, the cranium helplessly exposed. This constitutes no more than nuisance, as it comes from a later burial ground. More value has been derived from the slice they call Trench 4, with deposits dated to between the fifth and seventh centuries. These, according to the interim report, included 'a midden incorporating ironworking debris, bones and scraps of 5th/6th century glass imported from the continent .... This deposit was cut by a broad drain capped with flagstones. Two graves were subsequently excavated beside the drain. Both graves contained coffins made from split tree-trunks.'

Neat, convenient, ingenious – split a tree of sufficient girth down the middle, hollow the halves like the dugout of a canoe, two coffins provided. In Trench 2 they found paving, some shards of *amphorae* dated fifth to seventh century, as well as the foundations of timbers which may have been the 'corner and doorway of a rectilinear building'.

Most compelling of all came the information a few lines later on – and by now the rain whipping sourly over the grassy hills had begun to soak the roneo-ed pages of the report: 'Although the early Christian layers were not fully examined in the 1986 period, deep deposits were observed in the sides of later pits and graves. Finds included a broken arciform cross which had been re-used in a later building.' The report concluded that the same ground had been used over and over again for centuries. The Christian habitations seemed to extend beyond the ground later used by the Anglo-Saxon ecclesiastical authorities.

The Candida Casa at Whithorn, which Bede describes as 'generally called the White House' of Ninian, has disappeared despite the strong construction, 'a church of stone, which was not usual among the Britons'. Other investigations have located the site of the monastery, though the full extent of the settlement still remains in some doubt. It occupied the same grassy hill where the Trust polythene flutters, a little to the west of the long central street of Whithorn. None of the old stones from the original building is visible today, but descriptions have become available which explain the remarkable whiteness. Rough local stone, cut crudely into blocks, was set in clay foundations. Then they plastered it with a white or cream-coloured dressing, which made it stand out from the occasional other unplastered, dry-stone walls or buildings in the area.

From Galloway to the Farne islands on the coast of Northumberland, the journey cuts across some of the most remote inland terrain on the island of Britain. A pilgrim way from Wigtown to Lindisfarne – folklore picked up in Ireland – did not appear on any maps. Roads remain few, and had I followed the valleys of the rivers I came across, the Nith at Dumfries and, further on, the Annan and the Esk, I would have fetched up a long way off course.

I stayed on the main roads, Dumfries to Moffat to Selkirk, until it became safe to join a river, the Tweed, at Melrose. Appropriate, too – the first

Christian foundation at Melrose, many centuries before the Cistercians, housed famous men, notably Aidan, a monk of Iona, one of the leading lights in the Celtic Church. Kings befriended this controversial, saintly man, who became the subject and object of many miracles. His eventual successor and one-time student, Cuthbert, became one of the favourite sons of English Christianity.

The Melrose community – never as important as the parent house at Lindisfarne – originally sprang up on the riverbank some two miles east of Melrose Abbey, but in the driving rain and the drenching grass, the river in spate, I could find no trace of it. The walk did eventually reward me, though, with the first spectacular view through the trees of Dryburgh, where Sir Walter Scott is buried, and where the river has a useful crossing place and a hotel to stay for the night. I left Dryburgh mid-morning, and about a mile below the Abbey where a small weir fords the river I took the right-hand bank. When heavy floods come down it probably becomes impassable. Further on, the going gets easier on the far side, more level with long stretches of open parkland, and great houses and castles. The sun came out, my waterproofs became sticky inside. I had arranged to collect my car in Kelso, and then head for Holy Island.

Even in such weather, or maybe even because of it, the Tweed valley possesses amazing and varied beauty. An uncouth geological history threw the ground into many vigorous contortions; the dips and crags create a welter of ravines, combes and outcrops. Each turn of the terrain offers a new view. It includes the kind of great Gothic house which Scott or Stevenson would have been proud to describe, a tall gaunt building with, on one side, a tower or turret rising to a point, straight from the pages of *Lammermuir* or *Hermiston*. I know that somewhere ahead two rivers met, the Tweed and the Teviot, and I did not wish to be caught in their confluence and have to retrace my steps. On the fence, as I rejoined the road, farmers or stewards – the 'factors' of the landed gentry – had pegged the tiny bodies of moles, four on one strand of wire, ten dripping on the next, eight over there. The rain stopped and I moved out on to the road again. The Teviot came in behind me on my right-hand side, beneath high grassy banks, a fine brusque river.

Near the Teviot Bridge, just outside Kelso – a small town with a cobbled square – the rivers, if you face back the direction in which I had come, fork away from each other to right and left, and meet. The walk had taken four hours. I asked a man in Kelso the names of the rivers, just to hear him speak. The best way, he told me, to get to the coast is through Coldstream, which did not exist in the Dark Ages. I was glad to drive; along the journey – arduous to walk, since the land undulates tremendously – you see Holy Island far off, from the crest of a hill; to the south the rich ploughed fields of Northumbria, to the north the lowering skies of King Lear. In the distance the North Sea foams high, breakers of spume identifying the long low stretches of rock that mark the Farne islands.

The list of them reads like a schooner's log: Great Whin Sill, St Cuthbert's Gut, the Churn, the Brownsman, North and South Wamses, Clove Car, Roddam and Green, Nameless Rock, Staple Island, Gun Rock, Skeney Scar, Callers, Crumstone, Fang, Oxscar or South Goldstone, Glororum Shad, Megstone, Elbow, Swedman, Little and Big Scarcar, Wideopens, Northern Hares, Knivestone – to explore them would take a number of summers, because the journey to them risks life and boat, and the sea shoots up here in flows and scurries and there are no saints around to save foolish lives.

Lindisfarne is clearly defined by two citadels – a castle and an abbey. A highway must be crossed, the A1 to London, and a terrifying railway, by Beal, and then the causeway to Holy Island. 'Which place, as the tide ebbs and flows twice a day, is enclosed by the waves of the sea like an island; and again twice in the day, when the shore is left dry, becomes contiguous to the land.' Bede's description has been taken fully to heart by the local authorities. At the entrance to the causeway the Northumbria County Council has posted up the times of the tides, when it becomes possible safely to cross the mile and a half to the island.

Warnings heralded the way, stringent warnings, of the bridge's submerging, warnings that if the water reaches the causeway at this point one should turn back. I walked along the shore in the direction of Bamburgh in the distance, yet another Celtic fairytale castle, while waiting for the tide to let me through to Holy Island, and trying at the same time to get a better perspective of this flat, moody, long slip of land out in the northern seas. The forecasts of hazardous weather had their uses: the wind rose, to such a degree that it blew me flat forward, all fifteen stone of me, to my hands and knees on the sand.

On the causeway mats of green slime from the floating tide-borne seaweed spread across the metalled road, and the scrub dunes led off into creeks and shallows with waders, occasional grebes and an ethnic population of seabirds. No pilgrims at this time of year; the village had the air of a seaside resort closed down for the winter. The hotels were closed, tables piled in the windows, curtains inadequately drawn.

The Monymusk Reliquary, which contained relics of St Columba.

Iona led the way and Lindisfarne reinforced it, the way being the political power and statement of the Celtic Church, the monkish power of the Irish and Scots in western European Christianity during its early period. Columba emerges, whatever his saintliness or undoubted evangelical zeal, as a wheeler-dealer politician, as easy with temporal intrigues as with spiritual leadership. Aidan, who came from Iona, therefore understood such clout and in any case his appointment came about as a result of temporal conflict.

A Northumbrian prince, Oswald, had taken refuge on Iona while British and Saxon armies fought wars in his king's territory. Northumbria embraced the Roman, that is to say the English, that is to say the

Canterbury version of Christian liturgy, whereas Iona remained Irish and ancient.

Edwin reigned most gloriously seventeen years over the nations of the English and the Britons, ... Cadwalla, king of the Britons, rebelled against him, being supported by Penda, a most warlike man of the royal race of the Mercians, and who from that time governed that nation for twenty-two years with various success. A great battle being fought in the plain called Heathfield, Edwin was killed on 12 October, in the year of our Lord 633, being then forty-seven years of age, and all his army was either slain or dispersed.

Bede goes on to describe how 'a great slaughter was made in the church or nation of the Northumbrians; and the more so because one of the commanders, by whom it was made, was a pagan, and the other a barbarian, more cruel than a pagan; for Penda, with all the nation of the Mercians, was an idolater, and a stranger to the name of Christ.' In a few sentences, as the wind almost blew the book out of my hand, Bede thus sketched in the violent picture of Christianity in the days of the early Church in Britain.

After Oswald came out of Iona and defeated the 'impious' Cadwalla, he sent 'to the elders of the Scots' for a bishop. 'Nor were they slow in granting his request; but sent him Bishop Aidan, a man of singular meekness, piety and moderation; zealous in the cause of God, though not altogether according to knowledge; for he was wont to keep Easter Sunday according to the custom of his country. ... from the fourteenth to the twentieth moon.'

Whereby hung several tales. Not only did Aidan live here, and perform great deeds of charity, of chastening the rich, and of monastic commitment and self-denial, but 'he was wont to traverse both town and country on foot, never on horseback, unless compelled by some urgent necessity; and whenever in his way he saw any, either rich or poor, he invited them, if infidels, to embrace the mystery of the faith; or if they were believers, to strengthen them in the faith, and to stir them up by words and actions to alms and good works ....'

Role models: Aidan, Columba and the other famous abbots, priors and bishops provided figures worth emulating, a little below divinity but of feasibly attainable stature. The path to power lay in sanctity, and this interchange between political influence and holiness lay at the core of the Church's strength. Almost without exception every individual who gained power also had renowned capacity for devoutness. It became a benign circle: a man received power within the Church because of his appearance of immense holiness – and when he had power it became essential for the system to give him a reputation for sanctity, so that he could lead his community. The closer a monk grew to God the more powerful he grew – and vice versa.

The powers extended beyond the normal. Aidan performed miracles, not mere local cures and spells – though he received credit in the hagiographies for these too. Bede recounts how Aidan predicted a storm at sea and in advance provided the royal sailors with oil to pour on the troubled waters, which they did with the desired effect.

On the night of 31 August 651 Aidan died, leaning against a timber baulk in Bamburgh. (The village and the church where Aidan died were put to the fire by the warlord Penda; the wooden post upon which Aidan had leaned at the time of his death would not ignite.) On that same night, a young shepherd near Melrose saw 'a stream of light from the sky breaking in upon the darkness of the long night. In the midst of this, the choir of the heavenly host descended to the earth, and taking with them, without delay, a soul of exceeding brightness, returned to their heavenly home.' The youth, named Cuthbert, felt strongly moved, 'And in the morning, learning that Aidan, bishop of the church at Lindisfarne, a man of specially great virtue, had entered the Kingdom of Heaven at the very time when he had seen him taken from the body, Cuthbert forthwith delivered to their owners the sheep which he was tending and decided to seek a monastery.' Patrick, remember, had also begun herding animals, and archetypally ascended to eminence and sainthood.

Cuthbert, like Aidan, became the perfect role model – even in his chapter headings: 'How on a journey he foretold that provisions would be brought by an eagle'; 'How, while preaching to the people, he foresaw that the devil would send a phantom fire, and how he put it out'; 'How Cuthbert checked the flames of a house that was really on fire'; 'How he exorcised the wife of a sheriff even before he reached her'.

My wandering monk could have met him: Cuthbert reigned as Abbot from 685 to 687. 'So full was he of sorrow for sin, so much aflame with heavenly yearnings, that he could never finish Mass without shedding tears ... he wore quite ordinary clothes, neither remarkably neat nor noticeably slovenly.' He removed himself to Farne island, which 'lies a few miles to the south-east of Lindisfarne, cut off on the landward side by very deep water and facing, on the other side, the limitless ocean'. Cuthbert routed the devils who dwelt there; according to another hagiography, the *Life of Bartholomew*, these devils were 'clad in cowls, and rode upon goats black in demeanour, short in stature, their visages most hideous, with long heads which gave the whole platoon a disgusting appearance'.

Past the walls of the later priory, I walked to the water's edge to see whether Aidan's view of Bamburgh could have informed him that the castle had had 'an immense quantity of planks, beams, wattles and thatch' piled up like a pyre beside it by the dread Penda. The wind was in my face now, tearing the water out of my eyes, and still blowing hard enough to make me watch my step – 'a touch freakish today,' a man in the village said. Lindisfarne, like so many islands off these coasts – hard Skellig Michael, treeless Iona – has little lushness except for the tuftedness of the long grass. Unfamiliar birds, with long bills and dark brown feathers, swoop and then wander. The flora could give a botanist a life's employment among the mosses borne in on the wind, unimpeded, from Scandinavia.

The name Holy Island came several centuries after Aidan and Cuthbert. The medieval monastery and the later parish pay lip and eye service to the glories of ancient Lindisfarne and to Cuthbert and Aidan. Taken together, as the great pillars of Lindisfarne, both men made the place a holy of holies and had a remarkable effect upon all of Christendom and its mythology in Britain.

The miracle stories attached to them, however improbable, have their uses. Between the lines, mainly due to the tales of miraculous cures, glimpses appear of the way people lived. The life of western Europe, whatever the improving communications, had not risen stratospherically above the primitive. Illness abounded – women with headaches, boys with ague, people with distressed limbs and internal pain, dysentery and plague. In the absence of medicines they needed all the saints they could get. The diet included bread and the meat of sheep and poultry. They gave gifts of food – a lump of pig's lard had prized status. They drank wine if they were rich – and sometimes a visiting prelate miraculously made the water they drank taste of wine – and they made their own beer. They suffered terribly from the elements, and lived in fear of fire consuming them and their dwellings; their wooden houses dried out easily in summer, and the fireplaces did not yet have the protection of stone.

They wore garments of linen and wool, and, if they were clergy involved in worship, vestments of silk, coloured and embroidered. They travelled by foot, sometimes on horseback, though a good horse suggested wealth or royalty. People also travelled on carts, makeshift or large with strong, iron-bound wheels. Ill people seeking cures were brought on such wains to Lindisfarne. The monks wore boots or shoes of leather and carried sticks, and they used rafts and boats to transport themselves and their materials, either for trade or for building along the rivers.

Hygiene had not quite taken hold; if the body truly grew to be 'the temple of the Holy Spirit', it needed sweeping out from time to time. Cuthbert, for instance, wore skin boots and, in Bede's account, 'care of his own body was so far from his thoughts that he kept his soft leather boots on his feet for months on end without ever removing them. If he put new boots on at Easter they would not come off until the next Easter and then only for the washing of the feet on Maundy Thursday. The monks found long thick callouses, where the boots had chafed his shins all through prayers and genuflexions.'

Any visiting monk, whether or not he knew the Rule followed by his hosts, participated in the regime. They greeted each other with the word of God, and in the community observed a demanding routine of prayer and work. They rose at half past one in the morning; at two o'clock celebrated Nocturns; at half past three Matins; at six o'clock Prime, to greet the sunrise; at eight o'clock Terce; at half past eleven Sext, at half past two in the afternoon None; at six o'clock in the evening Vespers; and at eight o'clock Compline, to accept the gathering dusk. In winter these times altered a little: they rose an hour later, at half past two in the morning, and retired at half past six in the evening. Diet and fasting constituted part of worship, except if rigorous work such as farming or building had to be done, when it became necessary for men's strength to be maintained.

Avenue at Château St Pois, northern France. Forests of beech and
oak covered many of the plains and hills of Dark Ages Europe.

Seventh-century Frankish stele or stone memorial with heroic
depiction, designed to stand upright. The stele was typically used as
a funeral or royal commemoration among the Franks and
contemporary European peoples.

Simeon Stylites of Antioch (390–459) on his pillar. One of the early
hermits, he squatted for thirty years on stylus platforms high above
the ground.

Late seventh/early eighth-century glass jar from the Seine-Rhine area. The pre-Christian Romans, who traded wine with non-Mediterranean peoples such as the Celts, introduced vessels with new shapes which influenced European craftsmen.

Seventh-century French baptistery. The western Church favoured relatively simple architectural expression, and employed less ornate decoration than the churches of Ravenna and Constantinople.

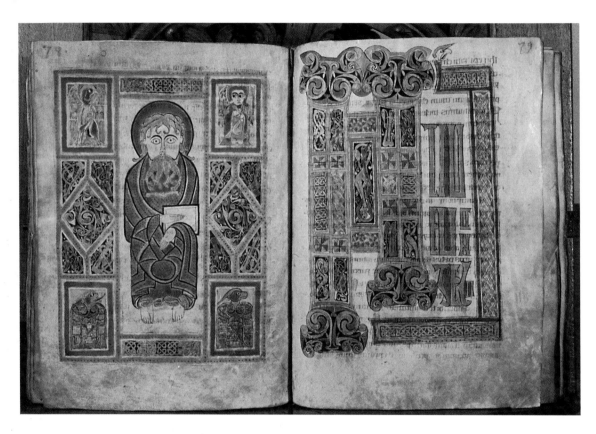

Beginning of St Mark's Gospel, in the seventh/eighth-century
illuminated Irish Evangeliarum from the Library at St Gallen.

Christ in Glory from the Gospel according to St Mark, from
the St Gallen Evangeliarum.

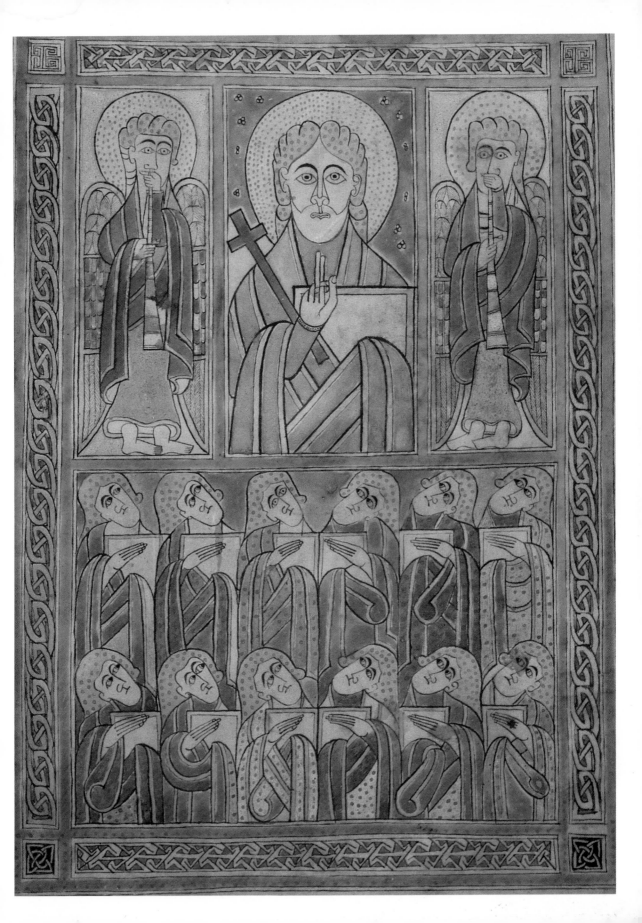

In 612 Columbanus led his party of monks over the rough terrain
of the Alps into northern Italy. At Bobbio he founded
another of the monasteries which made him so renowned among
early pilgrim monks.

As well as the famously holy monks, Lindisfarne produced one vivid, eloquent testament to the spirit of those Christian pioneers. A traveller arriving at Lindisfarne and sharing in the life of the community in the seventh century almost certainly had the opportunity to observe the *Lindisfarne Gospels* in the making. Some claim it to be the most glorious of all the illuminated manuscripts, a treasure trove of visual stimuli.

The book had four creators, all monks. Eadfrith, who became Bishop of Lindisfarne in 698, wrote the text; Ethelwald, who became Bishop in 721, bound it; Billfrith the Anchorite constructed the precious metal and jewelled casing; and some centuries later Aldred translated the text into Anglo-Saxon. The script seems certain to have been written by one hand alone, unusually in such works, and therefore it must have taken a number of years to complete, allowing for cold winter days, freezing hands, rheumatism or arthritic pains. It consisted of the four Gospels in Latin, followed by the translation into Anglo-Saxon, the earliest 'English' version of a translation of the Gospels. The book, intended for ceremonial use, was almost as important as a sacred vessel, occupying a place of distinction on the altar of the monastery, to be used on the feast days of favourite saints, to celebrate a visit by a dignitary, the remembrance of a death, the consecration of a bishop or the ordination of priests.

Eadfrith the scribe ruled his page and then wrote on it with wide-tipped nibs: strong letters, clear and flowing strokes, so excellently achieved that many wondered whether this style of script, brought to a high standard by the monks of Northumbria, had not been executed by Italians. In *Civilization* Lord Clark told a story which illustrated twentieth-century international cultural differences, a sad little tale of how much we have lost. A Japanese woman, he said, asked him when he met her, 'And what is the state of calligraphy in your country?' In the seventh century he would have been able to point with pride to the *Lindisfarne Gospels*.

These illuminations have a generosity and an obvious beauty, but put aside the emotional reaction and examine them for the state of man at the time. No morality appears: the primary purpose – the worship of God – has not been inhibited with visual or verbal opinion. Every intention seems clear and confident, and proceeds in a kind of muscular innocence towards the celebrations of God's word and wonderful world. Four of the major pages give firm attributions: '*imago hominis*', the representation of a man, begins the Gospel according to St Matthew; '*imago leonis*', a lion, marks the opening of Mark's Gospel; '*imago vituli*' shows a calf carrying a book and introduces the Gospel according to St Luke; and '*imago aquilae*', the image of an eagle, opens the Gospel according to St John.

Most of the other illuminations in the book are either abstracts, or portray the life of the natural world. All merge: plaits and eyes, legs and

St Matthew, from the *Lindisfarne Gospels*.

tails, whorls and dots – several thousand of them per page – and interlining and interlacing and spirals and trumpets and cross-hatching and fretting. If gazed at with intense concentration the illuminations effect hypnotic fascination, as the eye tries to follow and absorb each abstraction and thought suggested. When taken as an expression of worship, mild religious trance may have followed.

At this point the pathway of Europe not so much bifurcates as diverts, like God, in all directions and each one a kaleidoscope of possibilities. The famous plaiting and whorling has immediate Celtic associations, the interlacing which moves gracefully to a point and then returns to itself performing gentle arcs of pattern; the intricate mazes and arenas which overlap and counterpoint each other attach themselves surely in time and place to the far west of Europe, to the monks of Ireland and Northumbria who created – perhaps 'performed' has more accuracy – the illuminated manuscripts.

Until ... until you observe holy art from the east, from Ethiopia for instance, which, though an idiom unto itself, has the same 'Celtic' patterns in abundance and for good measure borrows from Byzantium too. Slowly the role of the monk in Europe, and the possibilities attaching to a wanderer such as the one I have in mind, widen attractively and excitingly, and the world, not Ireland or Europe, has become his oyster. The Coptic influence in the illuminations also confirms such far connections, apart from the known Egyptian role in the development of the monk – anchorite and monastic. The figure of the Dark Ages monk seems no longer merely provincial and insular, though thoughtful and devout, but a man who, whether in his wanderings or as a member of his community, made an important cultural contribution, widened the pool of artistic reference, and did so by means of choosing a life contrary to that of the way of the world.

Lindisfarne still removes itself from the mainland with the assistance of the tides twice a day. I walked a wobbly pathway along the highest dunes by the dishevelled lighthouse, past the flagpole with its triangular beacon emblem, the wind slamming in from the north-east. Some sheep grazed; there were a few fishing boats and one small trawler rested up on land. The crafts centre which advertised 'Lindisfarne Mead' had a sign which said 'Open at Easter' and a huge exclamation mark followed.

With the *Lindisfarne Gospels* in mind, it became possible while walking along the dunes to see the inspiration for many of the decorations. The sand swirls in the wind; the water shades from very dark to light and foamy; the seabirds, though less menacing than those in the *Gospels*, have, at close hand, an astonishing amount of colour in their plumage; and the mainland in the distance must surely vary in light and colour when the sun comes out. No sunshine while I walked there; Holy Island remained grey and still. The people had a silence about them, some sort of claim upon the past – or else they merely tire of the inquisitive face of the tourist.

The life of the monk or the anchorite in the Farne islands had much to offer emotionally. The weather and the low dull land and the wild sea, added to the thought, repeated prayer and occasional ecstasy of the religious life, took care of almost every aspect of emotional expression – from excess to withdrawal.

I drove along the coast by Bamburgh, whose castle confirms all the fairytale impressions from the distance, and then by Warkworth and Amble and Newbiggin-by-the-Sea, undistinguished and depressing places, except where the sea beats majestically. It had started to rain by Whitby. Through the gaps in the high-sided roads I caught glimpses of the cliffs which contain the famous local black jet. The harbour inside the bridge had been crammed with fishing trawlers, sheltering like children piled into a bed. The town has a resort's high boarding house quotient, but every place I approached either had no room at the inn or had ceased to trade. Eventually I found myself virtually the only guest at a big old house now becoming a hotel on the high outskirts of the town, run by a couple called Keith and Electra.

> Now we must praise the Guardians of Heaven
> The might and powerful intent of the Judge.
> The deeds of the glorious father, as He
> Eternal Lord established each marvellous thing.
> First, the Holy Creator, the Guardian of Mankind
> Raised up Heaven, as a roof for sons of men,
> Then the Eternal God, the Lord Almighty,
> Created the earth.

The words of Caedmon, the first author of sacred song in English: 'Whatever was interpreted to him out of Scripture,' wrote Bede, 'he soon after put the same into poetical expressions of much sweetness and humility in English, which was his native language.' By now Bede had grown into a most agreeable travelling companion – authoritative, involved, prejudiced, eventful, full of what newspapers used to call 'human drama'.

Caedmon had been a farmhand, ignorant, unlettered, and then he had a dream, that streams of poetry flowed to him. He conveyed this vision to Hilda, the great Abbess of Whitby, founder of Britain's most powerful, that is to say most holy, gynaeceum, who died in 680 and whose death her community mourned actively for ten years. Not only did Hilda encourage Caedmon to sing 'the creation of the world, the origin of man and all the history of Genesis', she constructed the most important settlement for women in the early British Church, 'and taught there the strict observance of justice, piety, chastity, and other virtues, and particularly of peace and charity; so that, after the example of the primitive church, no person there was rich, and none poor, all being in common to all, and none having any property'.

The ruins of the later monastery stand above the sea, visible from almost every quarter of Whitby, reached by climbing endless steps. The cemetery, in the grounds of the more recent parish church, consists of a forest of gravestones, all leaning in the same direction, clearly under pressure from the prevailing wind, all of the same colour, sand-brown tinged with black. The arched spars of the Abbey ruins stimulate the Gothic quarter of the imagination; Bram Stoker used Whitby prominently when recounting the life of Count Dracula.

Out to sea the waves ran higher and higher, and within lip-smacking of the monastery's rounded green lawns the waves hit the coast. Not another soul visited the place that afternoon. A curious light shone – the combination of bright sunlight and a biting wind which had suddenly whipped around to the east. Not a ship ploughed the sea, not even those low tankers which, for the last few days, had lain like long slugs on the horizon.

'At this time, a great and frequent controversy happened about the observance of Easter.' Bede enshrined Whitby's claim to fame – the difficult, if not very large Synod of 664. 'Those that came from Kent or France affirming that the Scots kept Easter Sunday contrary to the custom of the universal church.' Yes, but there was a woman in the case, Queen Eanfleda, who 'observed the same as she had seen practised in Kent' and this lay at the sting of the difficulty, because 'when the king having ended the time of fasting, kept his Easter, the queen and her followers were still fasting' – and, presumably, still abstaining.

It became a matter of moons, whether Peter's calculations at the moment of the Resurrection 'ought to be observed, so as always to stay till the rising of the moon on the fourteenth day of the first moon, in the evening' and, with various adjustments according to the day of the week on which the Sabbath fell, 'thus it came to pass that Easter Sunday was only kept from the fifteenth moon to the twenty-first'. But the Celtic delegation, including the Irish, Scots and Northumbrians, observed Easter on the Lord's Day any time between the fourteenth and the twentieth day of the moon, which sometimes led to them beginning the celebration of Easter on the evening of the thirteenth day of the moon, said to be earlier than the moment at which Jesus began the Passover.

They spoke harsh words in these Abbey grounds, an Irishman called Colman for the Celtic Church and the Englishman Wilfrid. Terms such as 'contemptible' and 'ignorant' and 'scandal' and 'prejudicial' batted back and forth in what diplomats call 'a tense exchange of views'. Bede's lengthy account makes wonderful reading, and from it emerges the impression that Wilfrid, being articulate and very well briefed, won the day over the more passionate and instinctive Irish monk, ironic enough in the light of the fact that what they all sought to achieve was an Easter which would be as close an emulation as possible of the first Eastertide.

'Colman, perceiving that his doctrine was rejected and his sect despised', returned to Scotland with his followers and liturgical history had been made. More than that, a point regarding evangelism had been proven: the rational, organized English would gain political control of the British Church even in the north, where it had been the fief of the less disciplined, though more fervent, Irish and Scots. It continued thus until the Reformation, which splintered them all.

Not difficult to imagine monks walking around the grounds at Whitby overlooking the sea, taking a break from the Synod and discussing with grave wags of their tonsured heads the spiritual and political implications of the argument between Colman and Wilfrid. With very little adjustment in language, and accurate costume, reconstruction would be credible. More dificult to survey and to judge emotional differences between a man of that period, exactly my own contemporary in years, and myself.

An afternoon of wind and rain on the heights of Whitby promoted a desire for comfort. Dinner at the dim hotel, and the birthday party which half a dozen girls from the town were having at the next table, with many balloons and ribald talks of husbands and hoots of 'birthday treats', took me down with abrupt candour to the real world, and the eventless journey in the morning over the moors to York.

Wilfrid, who out-argued the Irish monks at Whitby and about whom therefore my suspicions had now been aroused, restored the church at York while bishop there. His epitaph at Ripon, as well as including the observation 'He likewise brought the time of Easter right', goes on to give a glimpse of the life of a man for whom the title 'turbulent priest' might have been coined, who,

> In lapse of years, by many dangers tossed;
> At home by discords, and in foreign realms,
> Having sat bishop five and forty years

eventually received a saint's burial and reputation.

Unquestionably Wilfrid dominated Church rumour and gossip in Britain during the last quarter of the seventh century. His king in Northumbria expelled him, and again a woman in the case caused the trouble. The queen became jealous because Wilfrid's monasteries threatened to outshine the grandeur of her husband's royal trappings and buildings. His biographer, Eddius Stephanus, found his 'poor mind quite at a loss' to describe the church Wilfrid built at Hexham, 'the great depth of the foundations, the crypts of beautifully dressed stone, the vast structure supported by columns of various styles, and with numerous side-aisles, the walls of remarkable height and length, the many winding passages and spiral staircases leading up and down'.

Enough indeed to tempt envy, and hilariously the biography goes on to describe how the tempter, 'like a roaring lion' worked against Wilfrid. 'In this skirmish he [the tempter] chose his usual weapon, one by which he has often spread defilement throughout the whole world – woman ... she corrupted the king's heart with poisonous tales about Wilfrid, imitating Jezebel....' Great stuff, and it unhorsed Wilfrid and threw him out of York in 678.

Wilfrid's York has disappeared beneath the usual march of masonry, but one of his successes at Whitby has fuelled the popular image of the monk ever since (and further scratched at my irritating notion of times unchanging). Colman had been Bishop of York before Whitby, and he was, says Wilfrid's biographer, 'told that if out of respect for his own country's customs, he should reject the Roman tonsure and the method of calculating Easter, he was to resign his see in favour of another and better candidate' – Wilfrid, as it transpired. He, as a young monk, 'had an ardent desire to receive St Peter's, that is the Roman, form of tonsure, which goes round the head in the shape of Christ's own crown of thorns'.

The monks of Iona, and therefore most of the monks in the Celtic Church, retained a different type of haircut, one associated by their rivals with Simon Magus, whose magic had opposed Christianity in the first century AD. 'Upon the forehead,' wrote the Abbot of Jarrow to the King of the Picts,

it does seem indeed to resemble a crown; but when you come to the neck, you will find the crown you thought you had seen so perfect cut short; so that you may be satisfied such a distinction belongs properly not to Christians but to Simoniacs, such as were indeed in this life thought worthy of a perpetual crown of glory by erring men; but in that life which is to follow this, are not only deprived of all hopes of a crown, but are moreover condemned to eternal punishment.

The tonsure question had been causing trouble since the days of the anchorites in the eastern deserts, some of whom wore a long forelock so that God could haul them up to Heaven. For such presumption they eventually received the same abuse as Simon and his Magicians. In a paper on the subject the York historian Edward James makes the point that the old tonsure favoured by the Celtic monks found further disfavour since it may have originated with the Druids, who also used magic to counter Patrick's evangelism.

Dr James discusses the connection between hair and ritual. 'The offering of shorn hair to God or the gods seems to be known throughout the ancient world. Pliny reported a tree in Rome called the Hair Tree on which the vestal virgins used to hang offerings of hair; according to Pausanius the statue of Hygeia at Sikyon was covered with the offerings of women's hair

.... The rite of baptism in the Greek church included the offerings of the first hairs.' Paulinus of Nola dedicated the shavings of his beard to his heavenly patron, St Felix; a century later the pilgrim Antony described how on Mount Sinai, 'many people on account of their devotion shave off their hair and beard. I took off my beard at this place.'

The monkish tonsure offered public proof of the wearer's commitment: it echoed the crown of thorns in the passion of Christ and it marked out the wearer as a humble man, without vanity or interest in his own appearance. An Irish monk passing through York at the end of the seventh century would almost certainly, if not already prevailed upon, have agreed to have his hairstyle changed and would thereby have assured himself of an easier welcome at the holy places still ahead of him in Britain – the Lincoln of Paulinus, the Ely of Ethelreda and the Canterbury of Augustine.

If we accept the term Dark Ages as an accurate description, meaning that period after the Romans and before other literacy, after the brilliance of the Greeks, after the European world had learned how to express itself – and then almost forgot, as the barbarians had their day – then the darkest of the ages occurred in the fifth, sixth and seventh centuries, although by then the learning of the monks had, in places, begun to make the skies bright again. Earlier, the Romans had left considerable record of their world; the Greeks had founded the civilizing process called democracy and had laid down principles of thought and encouraged debate upon them. The advance of Christianity often seems like a response to a changing world – as if a spiritual power vacuum had arisen to match the temporal one the Romans had left in western Europe when they retreated to their (no longer everlasting) city.

In Britain, the local client kings and the Anglo-Saxon overlords contested the post-Roman power – to begin with in a rather haphazard way, and then in more formalized, regional structures, taking and creating kingdoms. Bede's *Ecclesiastical History of the English Nation* describes the country which the Irish wandering monks undoubtedly found. 'Britain excels for grain and trees, and it is well adapted for feeding cattle and beasts of burden.' My journey after York had to take into account the state of Christian Britain at the time, in terms of safe passage and refuge, and alongside such practical requirements, a logical direction. Given what Whitby had been discussing and Lindisfarne had been regretting, the destination became obvious: Canterbury now dictated the liturgy the travelling Irish monk would have to observe.

En route Lincoln, a Roman city, had been an established diocese, therefore an assured welcome on the road south could be obtained there. Always a priestly town, in fact: the Romans contributed to the cult of emperor worship in Lindum Colonia. Lincoln suffered some, though not all, of the ghost town indignity of other Roman cities in Britain, where the marble statues had either been decapitated and dismembered, or ignored in the general overgrowing. The Anglo-Saxons bypassed most of the cities and villas of the Romans, and the tiles and walls had been cannibalized in a relaxed fashion to build anew. In Lincoln the River Witham assisted the decay caused by neglect; as the trading posts moved away from the Roman centre, the walls went unrepaired and fell victim to the floods and the creeping silt.

I rounded a corner of the Cathedral in Lincoln on a foggy evening as a great fair thronged the cobbled closes. Pedlars and sideshows and entertainers maintained the long continuity of the marketplace's atmosphere. People with lanterns and brown accents bought food and clothing. Country people, largely, who had climbed the hill for the fair. The city conducts its affairs on two physical levels. On top of the hill, by the Cathedral (I had already begun to long for one cathedral built in or before the seventh century), little heavy trading takes place except at fairs. The commerce begins further down, supported by a large indigenous population of farmers, and the city itself now includes in its population the new commuters who travel a journey every day to London which, in the time under my consideration, would have been allotted the greater part of a week.

Travel on: Ely, the ship of the fens, did not then have the great Cathedral which now sails across the evening sky, but Ethelreda's sanctity had already inspired and invited pilgrims. Wilfrid's grey eminence had a part – delicately indirect – to play in Ely's foundation. Ethelreda, daughter of an East Anglian king, retired to Ely in 655 when the husband of her unconsummated marriage died. Five years later she made a political marriage to a teenage king of Northumbria who, much her junior, eventually chafed against her desire to continue with her virginity. Ethelreda consulted Wilfrid, who advised her to adhere to her holy wishes; her husband left her, and Ethelreda became a nun and founded the great establishment of Ely in 673. 'She preserved the glory of perfect virginity, as I was informed by Bishop Wilfrid, of blessed memory,' wrote Bede, 'of whom I enquired, because some questioned the truth thereof; and he told me that he was an undoubted witness of her virginity.'

Such purity nominated Ethelreda's body as a candidate for miraculous preservation. She died in 679, of a tumour on her neck, because as a girl she 'bore there the needless weight of jewels'. Several years after her death her grave was opened and the late Ethelreda 'being brought into sight, was found as free from corruption as if she had died and been buried on that very day'. The ubiquitous Wilfrid, still cleverly associating with matters of immense holiness, testified again – he had witnessed the exhumation. Ethelreda's virtues extended beyond virginity. In Bede's words, 'It is reported of her, that from the time of her entering into the monastery, she never wore any linen but woollen garments, and would rarely wash in a hot bath, unless just before any of the great festivals, as Easter, Whitsuntide, and the Epiphany.'

Is it my imagination, or does the Cathedral at Ely have a femininity absent in York and Lincoln? It came much later than Ethelreda, though her mixed monastery of nuns and monks must find some small echo in the pupils at the school in the Cathedral grounds. The light falling across the Cathedral, seen from miles off, has a different quality, a bright soft light, stoked by the gases off the fens.

The choice lay ahead – London, or Canterbury direct. Undoubtedly such a traveller as mine went to London, probably entered by one of the Roman roads, the one which became Aldersgate Street, and sought shelter in any one of a dozen religious refuges, houses or small local monasteries in the city at the time. The Christian Church had an uncertain existence in the seventh century. Not all of Britain had been converted, and Anglo-Saxon warlords did not necessarily respect the cloth of God that the priests wore. Throughout England, though unevenly, priests, priors, monks, bishops and abbots died violently, were embattled, evicted, banished, imprisoned or robbed. The uncertain state of the countryside, where a traveller could be laid waste by a wolf or a bandit or a plague, mirrored itself in the Church,

Illumination from the *Psalter of St Augustine.*

which had no divine writ across the entire country. Christianity had gained a strong foothold, no more than that yet. In 616 the Bishop of London, Mellitus, who had sufficient stature to confer with Pope Boniface and thereafter become a senior figure in the conduct of Church affairs in Britain, had to flee to Canterbury and then to France. A new king, Eadbald, 'proved very prejudicial to the new church; for he not only refused to embrace the faith of Christ, but was also defiled with a sort of fornication not heard of even among the Gentiles – for he kept his father's wife'.

But I live in London, and the place will little serve my journey's purpose, which had begun to unfold further. I had set out feeling somewhat at one with the idea of the hermit monk, 'the despiser of the world'. The contemplation of the man, and then, in my imagination, pitching him into the landscapes I had visited, where he must surely have walked, and into the monasteries I had seen, where he must surely have been a guest, mellowed me.

The fascination with his life and times grew – indeed it often had to be kept under control. Did he negotiate this hill in a cart on which he had hitched a lift? Did he sit by that river, washing his feet or his face out in the green open air? Did he meet, as in one of Tennyson's lines, 'an abbot on an ambling pad'? I had already encountered some of his difficulties, such as the contrary winds while trying to cross the sea to Iona. Even our diets had some similarities. As ever, though, urbanization provided the obstacles. Easy enough to stand on a windy hill in Kent, look in a direction where no roof could be seen (still occasionally possible) and presume that it may have looked very much the same in 687 , but where towns and cities intruded I lost him.

At the entrance to Canterbury Cathedral a plaque on the wall reads, 'On this spot Christian worship has been offered for 1350 years continuously. The Cathedral is built on the site of an older church which was used by British Christians of the fourth century.' Social observers say that immigrants congregate in those areas nearest their ports of arrival – which could make a case for Canterbury's eminence as the capital of the Church in Britain. Kent first saw most of Britain's invaders, good and bad – 'the landing place for nearly all the ships from Gaul', Julius Caesar called it – and the inhabitants had benefited from such close contact with the mainland of Europe. 'By far the most civilized inhabitants are those living in Kent,' Caesar continued, 'whose way of life differs little from that of the Gauls. Most of the tribes in the interior do not grow corn but live on milk and meat and wear skins.'

Six centuries after Caesar wrote those words, Kent received a visitor whose presence also penetrated and influenced the land of the Britons. Augustine, with forty followers, and interpreters from France, landed on the isle of Thanet, eventually received the permission of the King, Ethelbert, and from the house granted to him in Canterbury – the King had a Christian wife – began to evangelize with great success; in one day he baptized ten thousand people on a riverbank.

Organization guaranteed Augustine's success. He had been chosen for the British mission by that most efficient administrator, Pope Gregory I, 'the Great'; Augustine had been a Benedictine prior in a Roman monastery. Gregory, famously, had seen fair-skinned boys in a slave market, made a play on the word 'Angles', called them 'angels' and, having sent Augustine to convert their native land to Christianity, had several of the young men purchased for the priesthood. Augustine became a bishop, and cleared his lines of authority by putting a series of questions to Gregory, cunningly making the Pope responsible for defining how Britain's Church and faithful were to be governed, though along thoughts put in his head by Augustine. The issues he raised included how the gifts of the worshippers should be divided among the clergy, 'whether a bishop may be ordained with other bishops present', and 'How are we to deal with the bishops of France and Britain?'

Essentially Augustine set up a system of administration geared to retaining the evangelical fruits he gained. He created bishops along the lines of the guidance he had wrung from the Pope; Canterbury, where these prelates were created, became their reference point – the Pope copper-fastened its stature. 'But to you, my brother', Gregory wrote to Augutine, 'shall, by the authority of our God, and Lord Jesus Christ, be subject not only those bishops you shall ordain, and those that shall be ordained by the bishop of York, but also all the priests in Britain; to the end that from the mouth and life of your holiness, they may learn the rule of believing rightly and living well and fulfilling their office in faith and good manners . . . .'

Canterbury Cathedral's more luridly famous associations blot out the patient work of Augustine. The shrine of Thomas à Becket has drawn pilgrims since his assassination two days before the new year of 1171. The building, on three levels, rises above an undercroft, whose whitening stones feel as if they have some relevance appropriate to my purposes. Regrettably not; this building was begun in the eleventh century, which explains why Canterbury, Cantwaraburg, the town of the people of Kent, leaves me unmoved by comparison with Iona or Lindisfarne or even Whitby. I suspect some nationalism in myself, or admiration for those who held out for a long time against the general rule of Rome, and who chose to make their own interpretation of the Scriptures. Another, sadder thought: Canterbury represents the first centralization in these islands of a religion which also had centralization at its core. The monotheism of Christianity had replaced all the gods in the trees and the rivers and the mountains. It may have been more organized intellectually, but the spirit of man surely lost something fundamental when the word 'paganism' became a derogatory term.

My monk has come to the end of his British walk. In Canterbury he has found that he has merely reached another stage. He has learned that Iona and Lindisfarne no longer have the power to which they were formerly accustomed and for which Ireland looked to them, that it now resided in Canterbury. And having reached Canterbury, the power, he discovered, resided elsewhere, in Rome, and even then Rome had to observe other considerations, especially those coming from the East. He has had a history lesson, as well as religious instruction; he has seen places and people he has found unfamiliar, but perhaps has not felt a stranger ... yet.

O God, that art the only hope of the world
The only refuge for unhappy men,
Abiding in the faithfulness of heaven,
Give me strong succour in this testing place.
O King, protect Thy man from utter ruin
Lest the weak faith surrender to the tyrant
Facing innumerable blows alone.
Remember I am dust, and wind, and shadow,
And life as fleeting as the flower of grass.

THE VENERABLE BEDE
trans. Helen Waddell

CHAPTER THREE

DUST
AND WIND
AND
SHADOW

FOR A TIME, in the seventh and early eighth centuries, the figure of the Irish monk in Europe acquired a status near to that of a living saint, with his prayerbook in his satchel and his mind on his destination, visibly engaged upon *peregrinatio*. Stepping from a boat at any of the harbours of the period, from Etaples up to the borders of Frisia, such a monk set out across the countryside now facing me as I came ashore at Boulogne – more wooded then, beautiful and wide with rolling farms now. Today it offers few traces of the life of 687, and the local history of much of the landscape ahead has either not been uncovered in great detail yet, or has never been written down.

Although historians increasingly dislike the term 'Dark Ages' – since their profession is rightly invested in brightening them, letting in more and more light from the texts and the invaluable law-book sources of the period – the phrase acts as a useful shorthand. By comparison with the largely ameliorated society of the twentieth century, darkness prevailed – not just lack of information, but the darkness of ambiguity and uncertainty. Dark deeds abounded, executed by men whom we would now presume to rise above such things. Moral expectations had not been clarified – bishops, though men of God, went to war. Priests kept concubines, despite repeated threats of excommunication, and in some cases they attempted to circumvent Church objections and laws by adopting the concubines or making them nuns. The Irish monk's near-contemporary, Boniface, complained that many priests kept four or five concubines, and that, worse, this fact did not impede their chances of promotion – some became bishops. Even the taboos necessary to the establishment of clean genetics in a growing civilization still needed to be enforced by law: the declarations against incest had to be restated repeatedly.

The political and social super-ego of the time, in the country of Gaul-becoming-Francia, on whose shores the Irish monk had now landed, contained many familiar strands. In Ireland, the Celtic inheritance had given him an awareness of aristocracy, which protected itself by enshrining principles of kindred, honour and bonding, to be upheld if necessary through waging blood feuds and local war. The society from which he came resembled this one whose land he now set out to cross; it had grown along lines which in our eyes have by now become historically archetypal – family ruled by chosen leader, retaining territory, forming alliances, avenging slights which undermined the family's status, declaring laws which ensured continuity of ownership. Developments under the Romans had introduced a further concept, that of public service, the official as functionary of the administration. From the time of Constantine onwards those functions had increasingly passed into the hands of Christian bishops.

Therefore a society had evolved which had institutionalized power based on a ruling class of kindred, and it had retained and spread that power in its own extended families. Religion added a further dimension to society, in the emergence of the powerful churchman, abbot or bishop, part of the kindred or an outsider with a reputation for sanctity, quite prepared to accumulate wealth, quite prepared to defend it and his spiritual position bloodily.

I travelled from the coast eastwards to Arras, intending to get on to a good route through the kingdoms of the Franks and into areas which contained whatever little relevant history these Dark Ages had reluctantly yielded up. Curious place, Arras – the people, who seem flat in personality, with little trace of enthusiasm, maintain a town of lovely buildings, a town of squares and colonnades. The vans had begun to rig for a fair in one of the squares; the church, like so many others, proved too new for my purposes and despite the noon sunshine the temperature in the shade of the lane leading to the church dropped considerably.

After Arras I found a river, the Somme, and locked on to it, as an earlier traveller would have done. The same feeling of unease that I felt at Dunadd, that others have recounted from Culloden, multiplies along the Somme. The air overhead seems filled with the silent screams from the bloody ridges, a memorial on each one, from Picardy where the blood flowed through the orchards. Somewhere near here stands a hill which, as the archive photographs show, has grown appreciably in size in the twentieth century – not through accumulation of soil, but from the bodies of dead soldiers buried inside it.

I lunched in the Hostellerie des Remparts in the walled town of Péronne; local pâté, rough and open, *magret de canard*, some beans, a strong chèvre, a light local rosé, excellent. In Péronne, familiar names and feelings became available to the wandering monk. To begin with, the monastery, called Peronna Scotorum, had almost exclusively Irish associations (the name Scotii still attached to them), and the place acted as a rest and a staging post for the many monks on their way through – peregrinating outwards or homewards. In 650, thirty-seven years earlier than the date that my mythical monk was making his journey, the Irish monk Fursey, or Fursa, had died here and his cult flourished energetically.

Fursey had joined the ranks of these many 'pilgrims for Christ' and when he left Ireland, with his brothers Foillan and Ultan, fetched up eventually in Suffolk, in Burgh Castle, near Great Yarmouth. The terrifying Penda, a name from the Northumbrian lore, brought about another abrupt change in the political structure, and Fursey's patron, King Sigebert, was killed. Fursey fled the monastery he had founded at Burgh – 'pleasantly situated in the woods, and with the sea not far off', according to Bede – and upon landing in France moved eastwards, as I did, from the coast, though further south than my route.

From the fifth to the eighth century this region evolved from Gaul, to the kingdoms of the Franks, whose kings founded the Merovingian dynasty, to Francia. Fursey arrived in Neustria, the western third of the domain (though not embracing the Bretons). Burgundy and, in the east, Austrasia completed the *tria regna* of the Merovingian kings. He was welcomed by Erchinoald, the mayor, that is to say chief duke, of Neustria, who could just as easily have slaughtered Fursey, as he almost did with a local bishop – of Noyon – who tried to stop the people dancing and holding traditional local games. On this occasion, too, Erchinoald's better nature prevailed. 'He was a gentle, good-natured man,' wrote Fredegar, the Franks' historian, 'in brief both patient and canny, very humble and kindly towards the bishops, ready with a civil answer to all questioners and quite without pride or greed. So long as he lived he sought peace, as is well-pleasing to God. He was certainly clever, but open and straightforward about it; he lined his own pockets to be sure, but quite moderately, and everyone was very fond of him.' Erchinoald gave Fursey land to establish another monastery, at Lagny-sur-Marne.

Like Columba, Fursey built a reputation for extraordinary sanctity, promoted by, among others, Bede: 'Quitting his body from the evening till the cock crew, he was found worthy to behold the choirs of angels and to hear the praises that are sung in heaven.' Furthermore, Fursey was taken on an excursion by the angels, a sort of mystery tour of the cosmos. When they instructed him to look back he saw the four fires that would consume the world – falsehood, covetousness, discord and iniquity. 'These fires, increasing by degrees, extended so as to meet one another, and being joined, became an immense flame. When it drew near, Fursey, fearing for himself, said to the angel, "Behold the fire draws near me", and the angel answered, "That which you did not kindle will not burn you" ....'

Nevertheless, Fursey did not escape fully: he recognized one of the damned souls, whose clothes Fursey had been bequeathed, and since while on earth the man had acquired all he owned by way of ill-gotten gains, Fursey shared in the blame, that is to say the fire – which licked out and scorched him. 'Throughout the whole course of his life he bore the mark of the fire which he had felt in his soul, visible to all men on his shoulder and jaw; and the flesh showed publicly, in a wonderful manner, what the soul had suffered in private.'

In 650 Erchinoald took advantage of these legends when Fursey died on his territory. A shrine had tremendous uses – it drew people, motivated commerce, conveyed the sanctity of a kingdom; a cult made a region holy by association. Some nobles even created the cult of a man they had just martyred, on the grounds that they had been present when the soul was raised to Heaven. Twenty-seven days after Fursey's death, the mayor took the body and laid it in the porch of a church he was building at Péronne, until the church could be formally dedicated. When Erchinoald died, and Fursey's body was – predictably enough – found to be preserved from decay, Eloi, or Eligius, the same Bishop of Noyon whom Erchinoald had wanted to assassinate on account of his killjoy interference, saw the value of the cult of Fursey and squabbled with another local luminary who also wished to exploit the dead monk's santity. Eligius won, and in 654 set up a shrine in the shape of a small house at which the body of the monk was venerated for centuries. Fursey's peregrinations to East Anglia and then these wooded, watered valleys of northern France make him an ideal component in the composite make-up of the monk from Skellig Michael.

I followed the Somme to Ham, north of Eligius's see of Noyon, then turned north-east upstream with the river, to St Quentin. The history of early France is as difficult to unravel as an old path through these woods: to quote the historian Edward James: 'It has been said of France that governing a country with three hundred and twenty-five varieties of cheese is an impossibility, so, arguably, is writing its history.' My concern – discovering the past rather than writing about it – had to be contained at the modest level of any events or developments, or their relevant antecedents, that I could trace which could have had a bearing on my monk's journey; hence my route via St Quentin.

In the post-Roman, that is to say Gallo-Roman, structure of Gaul – where, even though the Western Empire had technically returned to Rome and been disbanded, much Roman political influence remained, and helped actively to govern – the invading Germanic tribes, Visigoths, Burgundians and Franks, dominated. The Visigoths had come into southern Gaul in 413 and established wide domination, with, eventually, royal palaces in Bordeaux and Toulouse. The Burgundians, under kings with names such as Gundioc and, later, Gundobad had, after invading Roman Gaul, reached agreements with Rome and in time established a capital at Lyon. The name 'Franks', as applied to the people in these parts of northern Gaul, no longer meant that they belonged to the Germanic tribe which had invaded by way of the Rhine. The term described the people living in the north of the country, who ruled territory other than that of the Alemanni in the east and the Bretons in the west. The Franks, a smallish group of families living along and at the mouth of the Rhine, eventually moved into a region of Gaul north-east of the main Roman military and civil supply road from Boulogne down to Cologne. The regime which came to be called Merovingian,

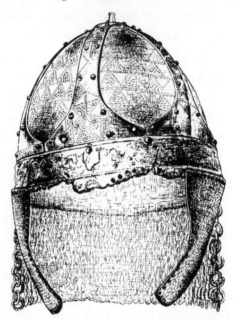

Seventh-century Frankish warrior's helmet.

through which the monk of 687 passed, began in the middle to late fifth century with the son of Merovech, Childeric, the first ruler who could with some authority be called 'King of the Franks'.

In the town of Soissons, through which I intended to drive after St Quentin, a Roman officer, Aegidius, had established his own state; Childeric assisted him in defeating the Visigoths in 463, and helped his successor in another successful battle against the Visigoths in 469. Both exercises meant that the Franks under Childeric not only had visible power, they also had the political wisdom to establish alliances with the Roman presence in Gaul, and Childeric's enterprise laid the foundations for the expansion of Frankish power.

Childeric emerges colourfully. According to Gregory of Tours, the sixth-century bishop and historian,

Childeric, King of the Franks, whose private life was one long debauch, began to seduce the daughters of his subjects. They were so incensed about this that they forced him to give up his throne. He discovered that they intended to assassinate him and he fled to Thuringia. He left behind a close friend of his who was able to soothe the minds of his angry subjects with his honeyed words. Childeric entrusted to him a token which should indicate when he might return to his homeland. They broke a gold coin into two equal halves. Childeric took one half with him and the friend kept the other half.

In due course Childeric did return, and married the queen of his royal Thuringian host who left her husband. She said to Childeric, 'I know that you are a strong man and I recognize ability when I see it', reports Gregory of Tours. 'You can be sure that if I knew anyone else, even far across the sea, who was more capable than you, I should have sought him out and gone to live with him instead.' She gave birth to Clovis, who acceded to the throne when Childeric died in 481, and whom some historians describe as the real founder of the Merovingian dynasty. With the same vigorous aggression as his father, Clovis continued to press the ascendancy of this collection of modest but determined Frankish tribes. He marched on Soissons in 486, an event described by Gregory of Tours.

'In the fifth year of his [Clovis's] reign Syagrius, the King of the Romans and the son of Aegidius, was living in the city of Soissons, where Aegidius himself used to have his residence. Clovis marched against him ... and challenged him to come out to fight. Syagrius did not hesitate to do so, for he was not afraid of Clovis. They fought each other and the army of Syagrius was annihilated.' Rapidly, Clovis imposed his will across the countryside and effectively created a Frankish dynasty. He eliminated all rivals to the throne and displayed himself imperially, using a combination of public show and deliberate cruelty to consolidate his power. He married a woman called Clotild, a Burgundian princess, who had been drive into exile during internecine power struggles. She, a Christian, ridiculed the gods whom Clovis worshipped, accusing Jupiter of bisexuality and incest. 'You ought to worship,' Clotild told Clovis, 'Him who created at a word and out of nothing, heaven, and earth, the sea and all that therein is, who made the sun to shine, who lit the sky with stars, who peopled the water with fish, the earth with beasts, the sky with flying creatures; at whose nod the fields became fair with fruits, the trees with apples, the vines with grapes, by whose hand the race of man was made ....'

Clotild then bore a son, whom she had baptized; then the child died, proving, it seemed to Clovis, that his wife's God was less powerful than his gods. She bore a second son who also began to ail, but according to Gregory of Tours, 'Clotild prayed to the Lord and at His command the baby recovered.' Clovis did not hold out very much longer against Christianity. In a battle against the Alemanni,

he was forced by necessity to accept what he had refused of his own free will. It so turned out that when the two armies met on the battlefield there was great slaughter and the troops of Clovis were rapidly being annihilated. He raised his eyes to heaven when he saw this, felt compunction in his heart and was moved to tears. 'Jesus Christ,' he said, 'you who Clotild maintains to be the Son of the Living God ... if you will give me victory over my enemies, and if I may have evidence of that miraculous power which the people dedicated to your name say that they have experienced, then I will believe in you and be baptized in your name.'

When the king converted, he renounced both his pagan ways and his aggression towards the Christians, and he began to 'adore that which he had once burned, and burn that which he had previously adored'.

The baptism of Clovis and his peoples, who also renounced their pagan deities, took place in Reims, at the hand of St Remigius or Rémy, who had welcomed Clovis on his father's death and written advising him on how to be a king.

The public squares were draped with coloured cloths, the churches adorned with white hangings, the baptistery was prepared, sticks of incense gave off clouds of perfume, sweet-smelling candles gleamed bright and the holy place of baptism was filled with divine fragrance. God filled the hearts of all present with such grace that they imagined themselves to have been transported to some perfumed paradise. King Clovis asked that he might be baptized first by the Bishop. Like some new Constantine he stepped forward to the baptismal pool, ready to wash away the sores of his old leprosy and be cleansed in flowing water from the sordid stains which he had borne so long.

The three-hundred-year line of descent from Childeric through Clovis, who died in 511, by then in command of all the territory between the Somme and the Pyrenees, led to two four-way divisions of the kingdom within 150 years. The second of these quadripartite divisions, Neustria, included a king called Theuderic III, the reason for my journey through St Quentin. At this point re-enter Erchinoald, who was kind to Fursey – or rather Erchinoald's son, Leudesius.

A brother of Theuderic III, another Childeric, had been made King of the Franks in the east, in Austrasia; his king-makers deposed Theuderic and exiled him along with the mayor of Neustria, a schemer named Ebroin, Erchinoald's successor. Ebroin's place of exile was the monastery at Luxeuil. The Austrasians then installed Childeric in Theuderic's place. St Léger, the Bishop of Autun, fell out with Childeric and was exiled to Luxeuil, where he found himself sharing a cell with his enemy, Ebroin.

When Childeric was murdered – along with his pregnant wife – for ruling too harshly, St Léger and Ebroin left Luxeuil and raced each other back to Neustria. St Léger got there first and set up in power with Leudesius, the mayor and son of Erchinoald. (In unravelling all this, Edward James's comment about writing the history of a country 'with three hundred and twenty-five varieties of cheese' strikes home with force.)

Ebroin gathered an army of followers, and, having agreed a treaty with Leudesius – who was godfather to his son – ambushed and killed him. Ebroin also captured St Léger, blinded him during torture, amputated his lips and dragged him, stripped, through the streets. Two years later he decapitated him. Ebroin thereby regained the mayoralty of Neustria and Theuderic was restored to its throne.

Then Ebroin was assassinated at night and his murderer, Ermenfred, prevailed upon a Duke of Austrasia, Pippin, to take an interest in Neustria, which had several changes of mayor after Ebroin's death. Pippin attempted negotiations and alliances with the Neustrians but eventually marched from the east across the countryside, into these parts through which I now travelled; be defeated Theuderic's forces at Tertry-sur-Omignon, a hamlet just off the Péronne–St Quentin road, about twelve miles due west of St Quentin. The battle took place in 687, the year in which my monk walked through. He could hardly have encountered a more significant conjunction of timing and location. The battle at Tertry became one of the most important moments in the emergence of the country we call France – ultimately it led to the eastern portion, Austrasia, having power over all the Franks, it sealed the eclipse of the Burgundians and the Neustrians, and it paved the way for the Carolingian empire of Charlemagne.

The prosperity here is tangible. St Quentin, though small, has an extremely busy air along its sloping main thoroughfare. The town possesses a river frontage where some boats had drawn up when I arrived, large flat barges with unmarked cargo, barrels and containers. The countryside has wide farms with mixed disciplines – cattle and tillage, and extensive drainage patterns, land worth warring over. The memorials on the hillsides, from two wars in this century alone, confirm the impression, though with different, international emphasis. All across this countryside the Franks fought their battles and carried on their ferocious feuds, against family members bidding for supremacy and against outside enemies. The power struggle did not distinguish between secular rulers and churchmen, many of whom, in the opinions of their later critics, merely used the garb of holy men as a dissembling stratagem, to create an impression of goodness. Then, when killed in the quest or manipulation of this power, they became holy martyrs, and their venerated shrines acted as assets in the aspirations of those continuing with the struggle.

The monk travelling towards Reims in 687 found himself in a civilization which had wide divisions – especially between those of royal birth and association, and those at the other end of the scale. The Frankish kings lived amid storybook colour and drama, as well as squalor and barbarism. At Tournai in the seventeenth century the fifth-century tomb of that first king, Childeric, was discovered. It contained enormous riches – a mounted crystal ball, a hundred gold coins in a purse, a hundred silver coins, gold buckles and bracelets, two heavily jewelled gold-inlaid swords, the king's battle axe and the head of his horse, and his signet ring bearing his face and motto – *Childerici Regis*. He was laid out in a brocade cloak, to which three hundred gold cicadas had been sewn, and their wings had been decorated with garnets. These were mistakenly interpreted as honey bees, and became so emblematic of France's early glory that Napoleon had them copied for his ritual decoration; some vineyards adopted the same emblem for wine bottle labels. Childeric's burial took place presumably when the king died in 481, or if it took some months to prepare – not unusually for such funerals, which sometimes took on the aura of local festivals – in 482.

Nearly a century later another royal person was buried at St Denis. Aged about forty and female, the body, discovered in a stone coffin during church excavations, had been laid out in a cloak of bright red, dressed in linen and silk, with stockings and garters. The clothing was decorated with two

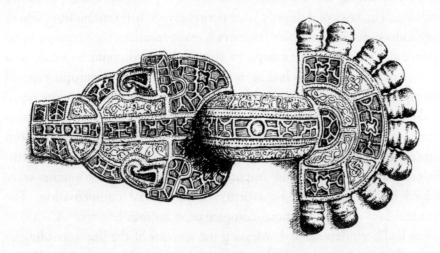

Seventh-century brooch with niello, garnets and gold filigree.

circular gold brooches inlaid with garnets, two gold pins fixed her veil to her long fair hair, and she wore ear-rings and a ring with the word 'Regine'. A large belt buckle, ornamented with garnets and gold, had been laid in the coffin. Her burial date has been put at around 570.

Other graves – of Gallo-Roman notables, of Frankish chieftains and their children – contained sceptres, javelins and throwing axes (one etymological derivation suggests that 'Frank' derived from a Saxon word for their favourite tribal weapon, the throwing axe), silver spoons and other decorated cutlery, swords and scabbards with jewelled inlays, and hoards of coins. Long before the monk's arrival, immense wealth existed in the ruling classes, who relied upon a treasury-based economy: each family with power accumulated wealth in the form of money, after the Roman fashion, or precious metals, or jewels. (Interestingly, from the point of view of Christianity, which sought to change pagan ways, old traditions of burial persisted. One of the spiritual roots of the lavish style of burial with grave goods lay in the belief that the deceased had not died but had embarked upon a journey.)

Such opulence gives an impression of gilded halls, with languid courtiers playing lutes, while outside, in a land of poplars and doves, the royal subjects strolled, the peasants happy in their ruddy-faced work in the fields, the monks singing in tune with the choirs of angels, peace and prosperity reigning. The laws of a slightly later period give a different picture; where they address, for instance, such matters as compensation, they supply a vivid picture of the past. For example, a financial award could be made to a woman of no means who had been raped; in instances of multiple rape all the rapists, if found and convicted, each paid their victim an amount equal to the total fine. The gouging out of an eye required financial compensation, as did the severing of either or both ears – whether hearing had been affected or not – and likewise the slitting of nostrils, the tearing of beards, the crunching of testicles, the amputating of fingers, limbs or tongues were judged by the courts to be worthy of substantial compensation. The criminal law applied financial compensation to murder, too. A scale of values had been determined, assessing the amount of the fine according to the level in society of the murdered person. It included large fines for killing children under twelve and women of breeding age, smaller fines for freemen and smaller still for slaves, both trained and untrained.

Trials of suspects were conducted in the towns and villages at regular intervals, such as every forty days: witnesses testified before important local people who acted as magistrates, advised by members of the populace who knew the law. A suspect could take an oath, supported by witnesses testifying to his innocence, or he could undergo trial by ordeal. If a fire did not burn him, nor boiling water nor oil scald him, his innocence became obvious. If a suspect or a witness committed perjury, they fell upon the ground and fractured their skulls upon the church floor, or they remained transfixed, as if turned to stone, where they stood. Conversely, the law itself contributed to the everyday cycle of violence by handing down sentences which required barbarism – court officers sliced across major muscles and tendons, cut hamstrings and cartilages, branded foreheads with irons, burnt the sexual organs of men and women by smearing them with pitch and briefly setting fire to them. In the name of justice they castrated and mutilated, and usually, as from time immemorial, it was the poorest who suffered most from the law.

The poor abounded, too – in smallholdings, in slavery, in twilit lives, no fixed abode nor employment. For every garnet, pearl, bead and jewelled inlay found in a royal coffin, as many beggars could be found in the streets outside. Some took the guise of pilgrims, wearing chains on their scabbed and half-naked bodies, claiming they had been condemned to wander in penance for some hideous crime, usually against some authority so far away that the facts could not be checked, or begging for alms so that they could continue their journey to the shrine of some saint, or to some distant reliquary, in order to cure an obvious ailment like a hunchback, or a twisted leg, or a fat goitre, or blindness.

Thieves and rogues lurked in this huge sub-life which thronged the streets and the roads and which, supplicating, shuffling and wailing, blocked the gates of towns and cities. Fifty years after our monk passed through these regions, Boniface, the Englishman who became 'the Apostle of Germany', complained ferociously that the brothels of Europe had filled up with women who once had been holy pilgrims. Most of those brothels predictably located themselves where trade might be briskest – cheek-by-jowl with the walls of the large monasteries. At the gates of a city such as Reims, long established as a centre of politics and administration, these motley crowds milled, accosting those arriving and leaving.

The contrast with the life on Skellig Michael, or in the rich plains of Munster, must have struck the Irish monk with considerable force. The stories he heard in the monasteries had to do with sexual and political intrigue, adultery and fornication, drunkenness and treachery, all across society, both lay and religious. Exactly a century before, in 587, Gregory of Tours had described how

there appeared in Tours a man called Desiderius, who gave it out that he was a very important person, pretending that he was able to work miracles. He boasted that messengers journeyed to and fro between himself and the Apostles Peter and Paul ... the country folk flocked to him in crowds, bringing with them the blind and the infirm. He set out to deceive them by necromancy, rather than to cure them by God's grace.

This outrageous charlatan 'wore a tunic and a hood of goat's hair, and when anyone was present he was most sparing in his food and drink. When he was in private and had come to his lodging, he would stuff so much into his mouth that his servant could not keep pace with his demands ....'

Another such 'impostor' approached Gregory 'dressed in a short-sleeved tunic, with a mantle of fine muslin on top, and he carried a cross from which hung a number of phials, containing, or so people said, holy oils'. He went to Paris where a bishop at whom he swore had him locked up. 'His stock in trade was examined. He carried with him a big bag, filled with the roots of various plants; in it, too, were moles' teeth, the bones of mice, bear's claws and bear's fat.' In chains, he escaped from his prison and made his way to the church of St Julian, where Gregory went to pray. The impostor had, he recorded,

collapsed on the stone floor on the exact spot where I was due to stand. Exhausted and sodden with wine, he fell asleep where he lay. In the middle of the night I got up to say my prayers to God, quite unaware of what had happened. There I found him sleeping. He smelt so foul that compared with the stench which rose from him the noisome fetor of lavatories and sewers quite pales into insignificance. I was quite unable to step into the church for this odour. One of the junior clergy ventured forward holding his nose and tried to rouse the man. He was unable to do so, for the poor wretch was completely drunk. Four other priests went up to him, lifted him up in their hands, and threw him into a corner of the church which they then fumigated with 'sweet-smelling herbs'.

After St Quentin I went due south, picked up the Canal de St Quentin and followed it to Fargniers, Tergnier and Chauny. Near the hamlet of Abbecourt another canal, the Canal de l'Oise à l'Aisne, cuts off across country past Anizy (superb food in the village *relais* – similar culinary standards hallmark the villages of Suzy, Danizy and Lizy not far away) and, skirting the forest of St Gobain, I reached the Aisne somewhere near another little farming village, Bourg-et-Comin. I could have gone with the Aisne as far east as Berry-au-Bac to join the canal which links the Aisne to the Marne – since I intended to travel down the Marne valley anyway. The river, though, had begun to turn an unhealthy white from some chemical effluent dumped upstream, a most disagreeable sight and smell, and time had run against me – too much lingering on the wooded hillsides, too much exploring the village churches, not one of which I found bore any relevance

Baptistery of St Jean, Poitiers, begun in the fifth century and altered in the seventh.

to the period in which I was interested. With some regret I succumbed to the autoroute for the last few miles to Reims.

The Remii, a large tribe whose name survives in their chief city, sided with Caesar and in effect betrayed their neighbours, the Senones and Carnutes, who had made a tribal alliance against the Romans. Caesar called Reims Durocortorum, 'where he convened a Gallic council and held an inquiry into the conspiracy of the Senones and Carnutes. Acco, the instigator of the plot, was condemned to death and executed in the Roman manner' – meaning he was whipped with scourges and had his head cut off. The Roman influence in the city can be seen in some ruins not far from the champagne suburbs where the signs on the walls of their cellars – Lanson, Heidsieck, Dom Pérignon, Perrier Jouet – read like some litany of social extravagance. Monks, according to folklore, invented – or discovered – champagne, and immediately turned it to the praise of God saying he had permitted them to 'drink the stars'.

Reims had been a centre of Belgic administration. Clovis (a corruption of whose name gave rise to the esteemed regal name Louis) had elevated the status of the city by being baptized under the hand of St Rémy himself in 498, and one of his sons established a palace here. Before that, Christian bishops had established a diocesan basis at Reims as early as the third century. The oil of chrism with which Rémy anointed Clovis during the ceremony came (naturally enough) straight from the Dove of the Holy Spirit, and reposed in the Shrine of the Holy *Ampullae* until the French Revolution. Both Clovis and Rémy are commemorated in the carvings which festoon the Cathedral's exterior. That baptism of the Dark Ages made a direct bequest to Reims: generations of kings of France were crowned at Reims right up to the middle of the nineteenth century. Rémy's successors, the bishops of Reims, became powerful among the prelates of France and ruled over several diocesan fiefs in a wide rural radius.

On my journey into Reims, where from afar the Cathedral dominates the eye, I had none of the encounters of Gregory of Tours in 587. 'There was a serious epidemic of dysentery in the town of Metz. As I was hurrying off to have an audience with the King, I met on the road near Reims, a citizen of Poitiers called Wiliulf, who was in a high fever and suffering with this disease. He was already seriously ill when he set out, accompanied by his wife's son.' Wiliulf died, and his wife married again, 'Duke Bepolen's son. It is common knowledge that he had already deserted two wives who were still living. He was loose in his habits and libidinous. Whenever his desire for intercourse drove him to it he would leave his wife and go to bed with the servant-girls.'

A few years before the Irish monk came through here Wilfrid of York, who behaved like an intellectual fascist at Whitby and who had made many enemies in Britain, set out on a journey to Rome. Effectively he felt obliged to – his power and wealth had made him suspect among his fellows and he had many enemies. The Archbishop of Canterbury, Theodore, from

From the basilica of Sant' Apollinare Nuovo, Ravenna: a mosaic
depicting Theodoric's Palace, showing the typical architecture of
the Byzantine Empire.

MAXIMIANVS

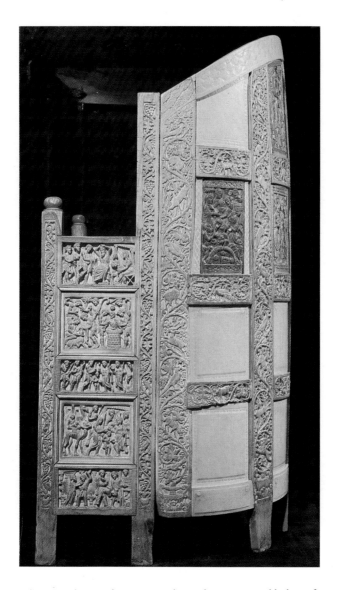

The ivory throne of Maximian, the sixth-century Archbishop of
Ravenna who consecrated San Vitale. The exquisitely carved
panels depict biblical scenes, such as the distribution of the loaves
and fishes, as well as motifs from the natural world.

From the basilica of San Vitale in Ravenna, consecrated by Bishop
Maximian in 548: the Emperor Justinian walks frowning to his
place of worship (above) and his wife, the 'actress' Theodora
(below), leads a procession of women to a portal under a raised curtain.

Mosaic depicting ships in the port of Classe, near Ravenna, from
Sant' Apollinare Nuovo.

Christ the Ruler, depicted in a sixth-century wall painting in the
Byzantine style: from the catacomb in Rome of St Calixtus, born a
slave, died pope and martyr.

Rome: the Forum. In the sixth century, St Benedict prophesied that
'Rome will never be depopulated by the barbarians but will be
reduced by the natural disasters of storms, earthquakes and
lightning, and will decline of her own accord.'

The church of San Lorenzo in Rome, built by the Emperor
Constantine.

Sixth-century icon of the Madonna and Child from the church of
Santa Francesca Romana in Rome. The Byzantine influences are
characterized by the gold ground on which such pictures were painted.

Tarsus, ordained in 668, had set out for Britain on 27 May with the colleague who had nominated him, Hadrian, an African prelate. They sailed from Rome to Marseille, and journeying up through France came into the power of Ebroin, the powerful Neustrian mayor. He allowed Theodore to proceed but detained Hadrian, suspecting him of spying – such was Ebroin's power. (One German historian has suggested that Hadrian was detained because he was black.) In 674 Theodore deposed Wilfrid, who then set out for Rome in an attempt to go over Theodore's head and plead his case with the Pope himself. Eddius Stephanus, Wilfrid's hagiographer, who claimed that Theodore was bribed to depose Wilfrid, describes a sticky case of mistaken identity by which Wilfrid managed to continue with his journey through Europe, eight years before the Irish monk came through.

Wilfrid's enemies, finding more scope for their malice in the supposition that he was bound for Etaples and thence by the direct route to Rome, sent off envoys with bribes to Theodoric, king of the Franks, and the wicked Duke Ebroin. They were either to exile him for good or kill his friends and take all his possessions. The Lord freed him from his enemies as though from the hands of Herod himself, for just then Bishop Winfrid, who had been driven out of Lichfield, happened to be on the selfsame route. He fell into their hands and may as well have fallen into the lion's jaws, for they seized him, took all his money, killed many of his friends, and inflicted the extremes of misery on him by leaving him naked. Luckily for our bishop they had mistaken the first syllable of Winfrid's name.

Wilfrid fared better. Several years before, a young prince, Dagobert, with rights to an Austrasian Frankish title, had been exiled to Ireland. In the power struggles of the Franks, when Ebroin seemed to be gaining the upper hand after Childeric's death in 675, the Austrasians, in the territory between the Rhineland and Reims, remembered this boy. According to Eddius Stephanus,

His friends and relatives learnt from travellers that he was alive, flourishing and in the prime of manhood, and sent to Wilfrid to ask him to invite Dagobert across from Scotland or Ireland and then to send him over to them as their king. This our holy bishop did; he made him welcome on his arrival from Ireland and sent him back in great state with a troop of his companions to support him. The king did not forget such kindness. He now begged Wilfrid to accept the chief bishopric of the realm, Strasbourg, and when Wilfrid declined he sent him on his way with lavish presents.

Unfortunately for Wilfrid, his return journey proved less agreeable. While he argued his case in Rome,

His faithful friend King Dagobert had been assassinated by some treacherous dukes and (Heaven defend us!) with the bishops' consent. One of these prelates rode out to meet Wilfrid at the head of a mighty army, intending, had not God intervened, to rob the whole company, reduce them to serfdom or sell them into slavery, or to kill any who resisted. Our holy bishop was to suffer the anguish of being imprisoned and reserved for Duke Ebroin's judgement.

Wilfrid talked his way out of it: 'I raised him [Dagobert] up not to your harm but for your good, sending him to build up your cities, to put spirit into your citizens, to counsel your senate and, as he promised in the Lord's name, to defend the Church.'

Outside Reims, on a hill going to the south-east, some entrepreneur has taken a World War I fort and turned it into a tourist attraction. In the car park beneath, juggernauts and their drivers sleep, beside a caravan which sells *frites* and sends thick black fumes into the air. The melancholy fort does not merit a visit, unless to reflect on the lives of the men who fought and were terrified in these filthy trenches; otherwise the exhibit has little visual, military or historical value. From the hillside, though, the land stretches out in a fine vista, and opens the way through the Marne valley. For the long haul that would eventually take me to St Gallen in Switzerland I joined the Marne near Epernay, due south of Reims, beyond the Forêt de la Montagne de Reims, a high and pretty wooded area with the smell of sawmills.

'A force of Burgundians and Austrasians set out on instructions from Brunechildis and Sigebert, son of Theuderic, to meet Chlotar. When Sigebert had advanced into Champagne to the river Aisne, in the territory of Châlons-sur-Marne, Chlotar came to intercept him. ...' The slivers of Frankish history, from Gregory and Fredegar, give slim glimpses of sixth- and seventh-century life in the Marne valley – battles and forced marches and ecclesiastical provinces, powerful local churchmen, abbots and bishops vying with the landed gentry for power over the people. In any house of these parts, where a wandering monk sought hospitality, the talk was of rivalry and kingship and Rome and Paris and bishops.

From Châlons-sur-Marne, where they have a museum devoted to

Goethe and Schiller, I followed the Marne through heavy farming country and many flooded fields to Vitry-le-François. Not far from the town, still travelling south-east, a roadside sign advertised a very old rustic church, though the century was not listed. Taking a chance that it might be old enough for my purposes, I climbed the hill off the thoroughfare to a village as closed and suspicious as only French hamlets can feel. The French must be losing their sense of *la gloire*: time was when a twelfth-century church would not have been classified as *ancien*.

From Vitry-le-François the River Ornain winds north-east; at the village of Revigny I asked a man who spoke perfect English whether any local people took in guests, passing strangers, for the night and gave them bed and breakfast. He looked extremely doubtful, and called his neighbour, the wife of a council official who worked in Châlons. She said, no, hotels were best, that round there the people had become much too wealthy to do that sort of thing any more. I stayed in a small hotel in Bar-le-Duc, where I could join the Canal de la Marne au Rhin, which led me to the town of Void – by name and by nature – and then to Toul.

The land journeys of my monk's day were somewhat facilitated by the continued existence – unmaintained but still marked by the wear and tear of travel – of the Roman roads. The legends of natural disasters, repeatedly told to travellers, heightened anxiety. A hundred and twenty years earlier a landslide had occured on the banks of the Rhône. 'Here a curious bellowing sound was heard for more than sixty days: then the whole hillside was split open and separated from the mountain nearest to it, and it fell into the river, carrying with it men, churches, property, houses. The banks of the river were blocked and the water flowed backwards.'

Long after this and long after the Irish monk, travellers were warning each other of the dangers of these roads thronged with slave merchants and their numerous stock, outlaws in the woods and groves, bandits in the hills. 'We advise you to use the most vigilant precaution in choosing a road,' wrote Lupus of Ferrières in the ninth century, 'for, in the wake of troubles which have erupted, brigandage is committed in the realm of King Charles with impunity, and there is nothing surer or more constant than violence and rapine [this, in the legally aware reign of Charlemagne's son]. Therefore, seek out travelling companions whose numbers and courage will enable you to avoid groups of brigands, and if necessary, to repel them with force.' Above all of these, the threat of illness hung most menacingly. 'When the plague finally began to rage,' wrote Gregory of Tours,

so many people were killed off throughout the whole region and the dead bodies were so numerous that it was not even possible to count them. There was such a shortage of coffins and tombstones that ten or more bodies were buried in the same grave .... Death came very quickly. An open sore like a snake's bite appeared in the groin or armpit, and the man who had it soon died of its poison, breathing his last on the second or third day ....

The landscape ahead of me now had a different feel to it from the Somme valley, a drier lushness, even though you would never have thought so, so widely did the floods spread. The dangers of the landscape in the Dark Ages are difficult to exaggerate. In the forests of beech and oak which covered all these plains and hills only an occasional settlement had been cleared, with a terrace of vines and land for some grain and pasture. Wolves abounded – local rulers offered bounties for wolves and their cubs. Villages grew up around palaces or monasteries, which had been located at river crossings or at high vantage points, such as the hillforts once occupied by the earlier tribes who fought the Romans. (All over Europe, many of these heights have had continuous fortified life – for instance, the Hohenasperg outside Stuttgart still has the traces of the fortifications Hitler built.) Travellers who had to sleep in the countryside, who did not get to a village or a house before nightfall, cut or tore swatches of briar from the thick thorn hedges and surrounded their pallets or makeshift shelters to keep out the boar and wild dogs and bison, as well as the wolves.

Bridges suffered constant wrecking from heavy flooding, especially in areas like the Marne valley where the land lies low, or further east towards the Vosges where the spring thaws of the snows pelted torrentially down the mountain. Some bridges could be replaced temporarily – as Caesar had done – by stringing boats together, but if this remedy did not work travellers either had to go miles further, usually upstream as the river narrowed, to find a ford or a working bridge, or wait for weeks until the spates abated. The greatest dangers came from brigands, bands of outlaws who lived wild and rough in the tremendous shelter of the forests and who slaughtered whole trains of travellers. Pilgrims, especially the entourages of churchmen, caried reliquaries, sacred vessels, gifts for their episcopal or monastic hosts ahead. Many of these had been richly adorned, made of gold or silver or both, as jewelled as the grave goods of the Merovingian kings.

The town of Toul had a benign air from the moment I entered the walls, at about half past three on a sunny afternoon. It has the status of a city, even with a population of about fifteen thousand. It grew up in the Dark Ages – it had a sixth-century bishopric – some fifteen miles west of Nancy. The Marne-Rhine Canal, the Moselle and the Meuse all flow in, near or around Toul, and the town gets its pleasing aura of light from this watered land; the countryside is strutted with little bridges. The narrow streets have old houses and small closes, chapels with turrets, gorgeous doorways preserved from Gothic and Renaissance times, occasional fountains, an old gaol and cobbled walks. 'Eight or nine previous edifices', they will tell you, 'were built on the site of the Cathedral.' Toul has serviced a rich farming hinterland with sheep and cattle markets for a thousand years, and trades vigorously in the produce of its agriculture – leather, cheese, woollen cloth. In the year 612 the city and the open country nearby saw great Frankish strife between rival kings.

Museums in small French towns have a special appeal – so often deserted or dusty, and the descriptions of the exhibits may have been written in pen and ink, in a hand which can only have come from the local school. And they do not hesitate in their chauvinism; the artefacts bequeathed by or commemorating a local dignitary will also bear testimony to his great virtue. (A museum I visited in the Vendée some years ago displayed a pair of epaulettes which had belonged to one of the many military sons of the area – except that this one had 'the courage of a lion, the strength of a bear and the demeanour of an angel'.)

Nothing so boastful appeared on the highly professionally displayed exhibits in the Toul museum, but the museum guard, a tall young man with an imperial moustache to supplement his navy blue uniform, followed me around, pausing at every exhibit, perhaps offering a word or two, studying me, and when I exclaimed or showed some pleased expression, nodding in agreement. He had an air of confidentiality, and frequently looked around to see whether we were being followed. I did not understand much of what he said, but he made it perfectly clear that part of his duty, as he saw it, lay in ensuring that I admired the museum and approved of it.

Who could not? A short catalogue of the finds on display reads like the monk's bag of souvenirs (or the impostor's bag of tricks): remains of elephant, bear, hyena, all found in these fields; a bronze comb from the La Tène period of Celtic art; a whisper of Byzantium in '*monnaie de Constantin portant le symbole du Christ*'; a medallion bearing the perfect image of a faun; coins with Merovingian effigies; river transport in the shape of what looked like a prehistoric catamaran, two long Indian-type canoes, with outriggers; fingers of Egypt – in fragments, masks and shards of Isis and Rameses; the pottery and bronze proceeds of the *Temple Gallo-Romain de la côte Chatel*, excavated between 1966 and 1973; drinking glasses and bowls of the sixth and seventh centuries, simple but lovely, with patterns and ridges embossed like slipware along the blue glass.

Then came a moment of sharp excitement: in one exhibit, not claiming any special status or advantage, sat a cross with the same T extremities as the crosses on the shore by St Ninian's Cave in Galloway. It had not been enclosed in an arciform, but it had undeniably the same feeling, the same mood as those in Whithorn. Of course it could have come from a European archetype, or it could have been a cross whose form had been beloved of pilgrims, or a design standard among the early Christians, or it could have developed in the morphogenetic forces which dictate that unconnected people across the world behave in conventionally inexplicable similar ways from time to time. Whatever its origins it closed a gap for me, between the heartlands of eastern France and the west coast of Scotland.

The museum in Nancy – a city otherwise inadequate to my Dark Ages enquiries – occupies part of the Ducal Palace of Lorraine, and you require a map to travel through its many halls. Large it may be, but Toul could give it lessons in charm and archaeological clarity. In a corner of the museum an antique frame contains a picture of a wandering saint with an Irish name. Fiacre settled in Meaux, an Irish pilgrim, hermit and misogynist – he banned women from coming anywhere near his establishment and encouraged other monks to pray for the damnation of women. He possesses a most interesting set of efficacies. Born in Ireland around the turn of the seventh century and dying in France in 671, Fiacre is the patron saint of gardeners, taxi drivers – whose vehicles were called *fiacre*, after those which formed a rank outside the Hôtel St Fiacre in Paris – and sufferers from venereal disease and haemorrhoids.

Outside Lunéville, where from a terracotta house blue bed-sheets hung out of the top floor windows, the emptiness of the French countryside gleamed, with a glimpse of an occasional shiny-slated château turret through the trees. The Canal de la Marne au Rhin led me a pleasant run, on lanes and byways, then back to the main road to Sarrebourg, a smallish market town, with some industry on the outskirts, though not the typical *zone industrielle*.

I parked the car in a central parking zone in the middle of a main street on two levels and went to a closed market in the Place du Marché. Here only two stalls were operating, selling eggs and cheese – large drums of waxy Emmenthal. Sarrebourg heralds the first taste of great mountains – any European traveller of the day heard warnings of their 'snowy fields and glacial roads'. Snow lingered on the peaks despite the warmth, and the rivers poured in full spate with the melting which had begun. The bridge at Sarrebourg looks down on a calm flat weir; the island in the middle has a mild municipal decoration of some small box bushes. The legend on the wall of the Place du Marché says that Sarrebourg's history began in the third century – and little more. The landscape around becomes interesting where it begins to be mountainous. Convoys of army lorries shook the little shrines of local saints; through the trees peeped exciting hints of onion domes on village churches. As I looked up through the wooded slopes, my blood chilled slightly at the sight of swathes of trees snapped off during last year's avalanche.

❖

If Wilfrid had accepted the see of Strasbourg from Dagobert, would the debates in the European Parliament here have the urgency and abuse of Whitby? The members of the Parliament, highly paid, travel briskly between Luxembourg, Brussels and Strasbourg, according to where the Parliament sits. Few try their patience by attempting to hurry legislation through. 'We may not have terrific teeth but we can do a lot of damage with our gums,' said an MEP. The architecture of the parliament building

at Strasbourg has a vaguely post-Albert Speer, Art Deco mood; busts of
Adenauer and Churchill feature around the circular walls. Time, and the
attitude to it, reflect the essential paradox of this unwieldy institution in
search of an importance. Every speaker, except perhaps a *rapporteur* or a
Commissioner, is limited to three minutes on a clock which lights up with
huge red digital nipples, and when the three minutes are up a bunch of

Tombstone or panel from a choir screen, seventh century.

irritated asterisks begins to flash. It may then take nine years for any notice
whatsoever to be taken of what those three minutes contained.

Despite many murmurs from the floor, we had no clear recommendation
of when Summer Time should be standardized. Innovation centres, latter-
day follies, would increase employment in the poorer regions of the EEC
– but when? The size of aircraft that may be used between regional
European capitals became the subject of a debate in which the Irish wanted
120-seaters but the British lobbied for their objection. When the time came
for the vote, the Irish adjusted to the English demands, as they had at the

Synod of Whitby, though it seemed likely that the decision would take longer to implement.

Strasbourg, the birthplace of Gutenberg, inventor of movable type, has a perfect set of museums, one of which contains the history of the men who hunted mammals when this town was a thorn hedge. Another, the Musée d'Alsace, which has gathered together the life of the hill farmers, has an unrivalled collection of faience ceramics; when the town was called Argentoratum it had a Roman ceramics factory – archaeologists have found a tile from it, bearing the name of one of the earliest bishops. Otherwise, the most powerful reason for my monk's journey to Strasbourg was the means of getting out of the place – via the Rhine.

The foremost man among the Helvetii, in rank and wealth, was Orgetorix. In the consulship of Marcus Messala and Marcus Piso, he was encouraged by the hope of obtaining power to organize a conspiracy of aristocrats, and persuaded his countrymen to emigrate in a flock, telling them that they were the best fighters in Gaul and could very easily possess the whole country. They listened very readily to his proposal because their territory is completely inhibited by natural defences – on one side by the Rhine, that deep and very wide river, which is the frontier of Germany . . . .

When Caesar, in his writings, praised an enemy, it usually heralded their swingeing rout a few pages on.

Basel, a dull place, has some remains of his much-quoted Romans versus Helvetii. Somewhere up above Basel, in Granval, one of the high valleys, Germanus became a martyr just a few years before the Skelligs monk came up the Rhine. From an old Gallo-Roman family of Trier, Germanus embraced the new monasticism of Columbanus; when he came into this region he found a valley with very steep scree walls, a fast-flowing river and lots of pools, a place which, even though it already had some inhabitants, seemed ideally remote for the foundation of a monastery. He widened the passes at the northern and southern ends and came into conflict with the local overlords who wanted to possess the valley in order to expand their own Alsatian territories. Germanus resisted all encourage-ments, whether hostile or friendly, to leave the valley. A band of hired mercenaries from the Alemanni swept down from the southern pass, the rampaging warlord came in from the northern pass, and Germanus became a martyr, though he had been just as secularly involved in the battle for the valley as his enemies.

Sleeping and waking, I lost count of the number of stoppages on the Rhine between Strasbourg and Basel, just as I lost count of the steps to the monastery at Skellig Michael – though for different reasons. The journey took a long time, too long. Other waters promised richer rewards, notably the 'high inland lake', Constance, across which two distinguished Irish monks travelled on a famous *peregrinatio* – Gall, or Gallus, and remarkable Columbanus, who conducted his men up the Rhine with a rowing song:

> The driving keel, cut from the forest – look – travels the current
> of the twin-horned Rhine, and slides over the water like oil.
> Together, men! Let the sounding echo return our cry.

> The winds raise their breath, the harsh rain hurts us,
> but men's proper strength prevails and drives off the storm.
> Together, men! Let the sounding echo return our cry.

To the refrain, chanted in Latin – *Heia viri, nostrum reboans echo sonet heia* – this big-spirited, crotchety, fearless disciplinarian entered Switzerland, conquered the Alpine passes and the river rapids, just a part of the monkish swathe he cut across Europe in the early seventh century.

Columbanus was routed from the monastery he had founded at Luxeuil, a deserted Roman spa in Burgundy, capacious enough for his six hundred monks. 'By the fourteenth year [609] of Theuderic's reign,' wrote Fredegar in his chronicles of Frankish history,

the reputation of blessed Columbanus was increasing everywhere in the cities and provinces of Gaul and Germany. So generally reputed was he, and so venerated by all, that King Theuderic used often to visit him at Luxeuil humbly to beg the favour of his prayers, and as often the man of God would rebuke him and ask why he chose to surrender to mistresses rather than enjoy the blessings of lawful wedlock; for the royal stock should be seen to issue from an honourable queen, not from prostitutes.

Columbanus further offended the royal household by refusing their blandishments and gifts, 'but he thrust them away with a curse, saying "It is written, the Almighty reproves the gifts of the impious. It is unbecoming that the lips of God's servants should be polluted with that man's dainties ...."'

Theuderic's grandmother, the legendary Brunhild, a formidable and lascivious woman who was Queen Regent of the court of Burgundy, held the throne in trust for her grandson, and from that position of power she dissuaded all serious contenders for the young King's hand in marriage. She encouraged concubines, who bore children, and when Columbanus so energetically condemned these bastards the Burgundians expelled him. They hustled him across France, from the Vosges to the port of Nantes, and put him on a boat for Ireland. Contrary winds grounded the vessel on a sandbank at the mouth of the Loire, and Columbanus took this as a sign from God that his mission to convert the Europeans had not ended.

He found refuge at another court, out of reach of his former enemies, and told them off as well for their immorality and hedonism. Eventually he took to the Rhine and led the monks on their prodigious coracle journey, singing upstream from Koblenz right into Lake Constance, which he and Gallus crossed and came to the town that now bears Gallus's name. Columbanus's forthrightness and messianic insistence on attacking pagan shrines and smashing their icons had created a furore behind him. He alienated the Christian authorities as well, establishing monasteries – such as Luxueil, and many others – without reference to, or regard for, the wishes of the local bishops. He had a personality which flowed over the reaches of his task, and therefore made enemies of the calibre of Brunhild.

Gallus and Columbanus epitomize one breed of the Irish wandering monks in the Dark Ages. They both entered the holy life through a typical Irish route – born of good families, off fat land, from the cleared and populated provinces, they became novices at a typical Irish monastery of the late sixth century. Both men had come from the same community, that of Comgall in Bangor, County Down, on the north-eastern shores of Ireland. The young Columbanus encountered repeated sexual temptation from the local women: 'The old foe raised before him the desires of lewd girls and young women, of a sort whose voluptuous bodies and superficial beauty stir mad lusts in the minds of weak men.' Columbanus ran, literally. He left home and entered a monastery in the west of Ireland, and in time progressed east to Bangor and thence, in his mid-forties, to Gaul. Like Columba on his passage to Iona, Columbanus took the archetypal, messianic twelve followers, including Gallus, and went into exile.

He had the good fortune to gain the attentions of a biographer called Jonas of Bobbio. The hagiography, a common literary form of the era, the life of a saint, local or national, expressed in radiant terms, constituted one of the few vehicles for intellectual expression. The intention may have been a contribution to the sanctification process, and perhaps for the personal gain of the hagiographer – none the less, as a genre it has served a useful purpose in unveiling the otherwise very Dark record of these Ages. The writer typically began with a denunciation of his own equipment for the task, protesting that he was rural, perhaps, and certainly ignorant. As he warmed to it, the tools of the hagiographer – adjectives and adverbs of uninhibited praise, extravagant subjectivity, vitriolic denunciation of all his subject's enemies – assisted him greatly. No compliment remained in its closet, no praise seemed too excessive, fact and opinion became as one. Even though flickers of the light of the times shine through between the lines, the hagiographies must be regarded as somewhat untrustworthy in almost all but the reconstruction of atmosphere. Columbanus's chroniclers exceeded the customary pious applause and told, among other things, of the (inevitable) miraculously attended birth. About to give birth, his mother dreamed that the sun rose from her breasts in a brilliant light, signifying that the forthcoming child would illuminate nations.

In the fields which reach high up above the railway track from Zurich to St Gallen the early summer harvesting had begun. The mountainside acres, which might not be expected to yield much, held little bubbles of stacks in a closed circle, not so much hay as high grass. From time to time in the trees above the track large houses appeared, some with immensely tall flagpoles rising from the front lawn, bearing the Swiss flag, the white cross on a red ground waving in the wind.

Cattle the colour of grey malt grazed in fields that had no right being as lush on such high foothills; every slope was an incline; every incline a steep gradient. Occasionally a village church with a dome hinting at the onion-shaped churches of the Balkans, like those on the edge of the Vosges, emerged from the trees. Deep in heavily wooded ravines, clear rivers, sometimes torrents, appeared, and the windows of the tall shingled houses, beneath the manicured edges of the woods, seemed unnaturally high from the ground – of sufficient altitude, perhaps, to stand above the deep snows. Tall, high, deep, these were the words that kept time to the rhythm of the train. In the fields, occasional sheds made of wood contained neat stacks of firewood, or hay for the cattle to browse through should they need a change of flavour from the green, juicy grass.

In the Dark Ages a pathway such as this, which ran like a natural fault, a winding terrace, along the hill, held substantial perils – timber wolves, alpine cats and bears. Columbanus, walking in similar terrain, reached the mouth of a cave whose inhabitant, a brown bear, menaced him. Columbanus told him off, saying he wanted the cave to meditate in and worship God.

The railway station shone as clean as the legends of modern Switzerland. In the Altstadt, by the Cathedral, I came to the Gallus-Strasse and the collection of large buildings which stand at the heart and soul of St Gallen – the Stiftsbibliothek, the Abbey Library, a relict of the old Benedictine monastery and now protected by Church and State alike. An usher took my arm and led me back to the corridor outside the Library room where, ranged in rows along the floor by the wall, like quiet stalls of small furry animals, lay large slippers, galoshes made of felt, in grey and beige. Patiently he assisted me to slip a pair on over my shoes.

The Library at St Gallen has great beauty, on a par with, say, the Queen's College in Oxford. The surprisingly small room gives an immediate impression of brown chocolate-and-gilt baroque, in simple rounded designs, bookcases and bulging stacks, all pleasingly harmonized in a honey light, the floor now highly polished by the generations of felt clogs. The only manuscript on view whose work was remotely contemporary with 687 sat in a case in the middle of the floor, catalogued as '*Irisches Evangeliarum – geschrieben und gemalt von Iren um 750*' – Irish Gospels written and illuminated by Irishmen about 750. It had the same faces that peeped out of the *Lindisfarne Gospels*, and the same perspective appeared in the figures – the impossibly long fingers, the cunning animal entrapped in long spars of design, more dots travelling down the length of the long designs, within the controlling lines and the foreshortened views.

The whorling and skeining along the margins might have come from the Northumbrian illuminations and, as with all the great books of the era, the colour bathed the prayers, gentle, lit with rich pigments made from plant dyes and drawn carefully by a loving hand with no long tradition of handwriting or painting. Where the tourists shuffled around in the big felt overshoes, the gilt and brown bow-fronted cabinets and cases contained lives, biographies – usually hagiographies – of Gallus and his successor Otmar, as well as copies of the Rule of Columbanus and Benedict. The Library relates generally to a much later period, when the incunabulae preserved here were created in the middle of the high period of European Christian manuscript illumination.

Gallus should have gone on into Italy over the Alps with the curmudgeonly Columbanus, but his age and a fever prevented him and he became a hermit, partly in response to Columbanus's admonition of him – despite his great age and sickness – for his tardiness, his not being able to walk over the mountains. 'Equal your equals' became a motto with Columbanus, and when monks did not work hard enough he condemned them to a year's illness: 'No man shall sleep until he has tired himself enough to sleep on his feet.' Gallus's punishment for being old and infirm specified that he could never celebrate Mass again during Columbanus's lifetime. He did, however, create enough of a reputation for sanctity in his cell near the town that now bears his name to draw many visitors, and to cause a Benedictine monastery to be established after his death.

Gallus refused all offers from local potentates of bishoprics or abbacies; a hermit he became and a hermit he stayed, discomfited by the punishment of Columbanus. A big and awkward man, he sometimes left his hermit's cell and walked, preaching, through eastern Switzerland. He outlived Columbanus by fifteen years, and when Columbanus died in Bobbio in 615 his monks sent Gallus the pastoral staff, a wooden crozier, which Columbanus had carried, as a sign that Gallus had now been released from Columbanus's censure.

Gallus lived gently in his hermitage. His legends also ran true to the traditional hagiographical form: he banished the demon of the waters who formed an alliance with the demon of the mountains to drive him out. He built his hut by the River Steinach because he stumbled and fell in the undergrowth, and the fall revealed to him a small, secluded and welcoming clearing on the riverbank. A bear roared into this woodland oasis; Gallus bade him put a log on the fire and rewarded the bear with bread (the legend appears on some versions of the town crest). Where Columbanus used aggressive denunciation and insistence upon rote and the most emphatic interpretations of the word of God, Gallus used persuasion and diplomacy and made friends, not enemies, of the ruling classes.

His quieter stature drew many to the place he lived in, and the numbers of pilgrims increased after his death as his reputation grew. His town keeps an awareness of him alive; hymns and songs composed in his honour after his death are displayed in the Library. His place in the canon of Irish monks who evangelized in Europe stands perhaps second to that of Columbanus, and above that of the many others: Colman, who went to Austria; Deicola, who dropped out of Columbanus's band when the great man was arrested and went to live in a hut in the forest that also grew to a monastery; Fiacre, whom I encountered in the museum at Nancy; Fridolin of Glarus; Fridian, who established his monastery in Tuscany at Lucca and became known as San Frediano; Fursey, whose memory is venerated in Péronne; Kilian, who also travelled along the Rhine and met a violent death in Franconia. The list grew so long that their presence in Europe in the sixth and seventh centuries can be counted as a cultural and religious invasion. Many of them still retain a place in the liturgical calendars of France, Italy, Switzerland and Germany as well as their native Ireland. They held on for as long as they could to the liturgy of the Celtic Church in matters such as the timing of Easter and the tonsure, and their influence in the monasteries continued, with reinforcements, for several centuries.

Downward the various goddess took her flight
And drew a thousand colours from the light.

VIRGIL *Aeneid*
trans. John Dryden

CHAPTER FOUR

THE MANY
COLOURS
OF
THE LIGHT

I N DUE COURSE Columbanus had to leave Switzerland. Attacks made upon him and his followers had escalated intolerably, and he lost produce, animals, buildings and followers in burning, slaughtering raids by neighbours whom he had offended. He left with a bad grace: 'We found a golden egg, but it contained serpents,' he said as he hiked with his party – without Gallus – over the mountains into Lombardy and founded his last monastery at Bobbio.

The Library at St Gallen contains a ninth-century copy of Columbanus's Rule, the austere regime which he laid down for his monks. Those innumerable holy peregrinators who travelled routes like mine, even those who never made it to sainthood – the *Liber Memoriales* in Reichenau contains lists of pilgrims' names like a visitors' book – were expected to fall in with the regimen while accepting a monastery's hospitality. It seems inconceivable that a martinet such as Columbanus would permit anyone to stay under his roof who would not attempt to harmonize with his rigorous theme. Privation took precedence, a belief that stringency led to spiritual improvement, the only goal. He insisted on maintaining a heightened awareness of death, that the brief mortal span had been allotted only to enhance the glory of the Creator, and that to this end human beings while on earth had only the tenancy of a guest: 'Think about death. Then will pleasure and amusement, desire and luxury fall silent; then will the body lie rotting in the earth.'

The Rule stipulated a complete rejection of sensuality in all but the most unavoidable forms of sensations – such as a fine morning, or a succulent fruit – all of which in any case had to be turned to the praise of God. Columbanan monks had to eschew every personal possession: the Rule demanded asceticism in diet, alternating between plain food and fasting: 'The food of monks will be plain – cabbage, vegetables, flour mixed with water unto a biscuit, all to be consumed in the evening.' Work guided prayer and vice versa: his disciplines resembled those of earlier Irish monastic rules: 'The wise man's work is in his mouth; the unlearned work with their hands.' He also demanded utter obedience: 'Do not disagree, even in your mind, do not speak as you please, do not go anywhere with total freedom.' Punishment was the custodian of obedience and it played a leading role. 'Love the good men,' Columbanus proclaimed, 'but treat the dishonest harshly.' A monk who spoke at table received six strokes of a cane, as did a monk caught laughing at prayers. The man who did not sing as well as he should, even though 'through a cough', also received six strokes, and for gossip or lies or contradicting superiors the number of strokes went up to fifty. Penitential in stated intent, he therefore imposed upon all wills their contrary tendency: 'The talkative person is to be sentenced to silence, the disturber to gentleness, the sleepy fellow to watchfulness.'

The typical legends of miracles and sanctity grew up around Columbanus. He had a particular efficacy in the animal kingdom. As well as subduing the bear in the cave, he won a psychological victory over a pack of wolves who nuzzled his robe and departed; the squirrels warmed themselves on his breast, and he scarcely needed to sew the nets he and Gallus fished with in Lake Constance, since the fish leaped to his outstretched hand on the bank of the lake. He dominated his communities in the monasteries he founded at Annegray on the lower slopes of the Vosges, on the Burgundy–Austrasia border, at Luxeuil ten miles away and finally at Bobbio in Italy, on a tributary of the Po. His followers multiplied and, taking inspiration from his harsh but powerful style, spread his Rule on both sides of the Alps in France and northern Italy. Estimates compiled from his own works, from those of his biographers, from contemporary sources and from historians suggest that by the end of the seventh century up to sixty monasteries had been founded across France and Switzerland by Columbanan-trained religious. Two centuries later a writer, Adso of Montier, still humming with wonder at Columbanus's achievements, observed, 'And now what place, what city, does not rejoice in having for its ruler a bishop or an abbot trained in the discipline of that holy man? For it is certain that by virtue of his authority, almost the whole land of the Franks has been for the first time properly furnished with regular institutions.'

Columbanus wrote Latin verse, some of it in a light vein, and it was he who brought to the continent the Irish version of Easter and the Irish tonsure, both of which were later conceded at Whitby. His image survives powerfully – tall and aggressive, an impression of brute endurance traversing France not once but twice, exhorting his monks to row hard and rhythmically against the mighty current of the Rhine and finally stalking determinedly through the Alpine passes until he emerged into the sunlit plains of Lombardy in 612. For every monkish missionary of the Dark Ages and for many since then – even for modern pilgrims – the image of Columbanus remained inspirational, with his 'pastoral' staff (to ward off attackers); his holy book, one he was either writing or reading, borne in a leather bag that had been steeped in wax to make it waterproof; perhaps assorted relics either brought from Ireland or gleaned from shrines along the way; consecrated hosts in special small wallets for Last Rites or in the event of being only able to celebrate Communion; and, where exception-ally fortunate, a spare pair of shoes or sandals.

As I followed in my own monk's footsteps, obvious temptations threatened to divert me – to visit all the shrines of the Irish *peregrinii* in northern Italy: Lucca of San Frediano, Aosta where the 'man of wondrous power', Orso, became a bishop in the late sixth century, and Columbanus's Bobbio. But in the event the light coming from the East offered newer wonders, and I set my sights on Ravenna. I made careful enquiries about the possibility of walking through the Alps to St Moritz and down into Italy, aiming for Como and then Brescia. My admiration for Columbanus grew further: in his day only the fearless, the desperate or the mad braved the Alps – in summer the brigands made up for any of the dangers that had been alleviated by improved weather.

If it had been Columbanus's intention to found yet another monastery in line with the ambition stated in his own works – 'The salvation of many souls and a solitary spot of my own' – then he must have had a team of bearers, probably the monks themselves, and whatever his obsession with

Bronze gilt plaque, probably Lombard, *c.* 600.

the denial of possessions they required some luggage, which made for difficult hauling over the rocky passes. Yes, said a precise Swiss Alpine guide, ancient walking paths did exist in the Alps, very old, many centuries. Thirteen centuries? He said that if I was asking him had these been missionary paths, he did not know, since he was not a historian. Yes, it would have been possible, he said, to walk these mountains in those days. I asked him how long I should allow to make such a walk and he said, pursing his lips, 'To Brescia – or Como?' and looking at my clothes added, 'No insult, please, but you are not dressed well.' I took it that he meant not dressed appropriately for the mountains. 'With boots and pack it would take – for you – one month allowing for safety and resting.' Therefore in 612, in who knows what kind of weather, in robes and sandals, praying and chanting psalms along the path, Columbanus's journey shakes the imagination: he was in his early seventies.

From St Gallen, by a series of small trains and buses I joined the Rhine where it came out of Lake Constance, and stayed with it as far as Chur; more public transport, another of the long high trains, and down to Lugano, to a hectically busy station full of schoolchildren and university students on their way home for the weekend, and then a half-hour train journey to spend Friday night in Como amid a spectacular lightning storm. The banks of Lake Como range in terraces up to high bushy hills which are sprinkled heavily with white and ochre villas owning boats at the water's edge. Hitler wanted Como for his own toy when his conquest of Europe had been completed, just as he wanted Oxford as his capital of Britain. The Romans got to Como first and gave it an important regional position. The silk trade flourished here, and now the town's hotels had filled with textile and furniture people attending a fair in Milan. In the seventh century it sat on the edge of an area of turmoil, where the Lombards ruled.

'They shaved the neck, and left it bare up to the back of the head, having their hair hanging down on the face as far as the mouth and parting it on either side by a part in the forehead.' Paul the Deacon, born during the Skelligs' monk's lifetime, though thirty years after he passed through Lombardy, wrote *Historia Langobardum*, the widely influential history of the Lombards. 'Their garments were mostly loose and linen, such as the Anglo-Saxons are wont to wear [historians have claimed this as the first appearance of the term "Anglo-Saxon" in print], ornamented with broad borders woven in various colours. Their shoes, indeed, were open almost to the tip of the great toe, and were held on by shoe latchets interlacing alternately. But later they began to wear trousers over which they put leggings of shaggy woollen cloth when they rode.'

Paul, of vague birth date, somewhere between 720 and 730, was descended from an oppressed family of Lombard aristocrats, and wrote his great work at the end of the eighth century largely while living in the southern Italian monastery of Monte Cassino. He already had a reputation as a historian, as a man of good character beloved of his fellow monks – 'he had every good quality at one and the same time' – and with pronounced, and for the time revolutionary, ideas about the raising of young people. 'Act with moderation and do not birch them, or they will return to their beastliness after correction. A master who in his anger reprimands a child beyond measure should be pacified and corrected. Strong-arm methods may render a child naughtier than ever.' He also suggested that 'to make the children strong and satisfy their natural requirements of relaxation and high

Gilded copper relief, part of a Lombard helmet decoration.

spirits they should, at the discretion of their teachers, be sent each week or month into a park or some open field where they can play for one hour, under the watchful eye of their teachers.' On closer examination the suggestion does not seem at such odds with the kind of regime required in Paul's monastic environment: parents seeking prestige willingly gave up their children to God – and from very young ages, from four onwards. The acceptance of the child in the monastery school may have required a donation from the parents to the abbot, and in rich, successful foundations a visiting monk would have met whole groups of small children.

Paul's history of the Lombards refers to ancient historical sources such as Pliny in order to place the Lombards geographically, which he does as coming from the place he calls 'Scadinavia' (*sic*), but which in reality probably meant northern Germany, and indeed he does lump the Lombards together with Goths, Vandals 'and also other fierce and barbarous nations [that] have come from Germany'.

They migrated under the tribal name of Winnili, meaning 'the people from the meadowlands', or, in another attribution, 'those eager for war', and their name changed as they came south. 'It is certain, however, that the Langobards were afterwards so called on account of the length of their beards untouched by the knife, whereas they had first been called Winnili; for according to their language "lang" means "long" and "bart" means "beard".' After generations of depredating migrations, including ravages towards the east of Europe into the Hungarian Plain, they came in 568 into the valley of the River Po under their hero-king Alboin, who married the daughter of Chlothar, the King of the Franks. After she died Alboin married Rosemund, daughter of the slain king of another Germanic tribe, the Gepidae, in whose conquest Alboin had his finest hour – and it led to his last.

'After this king had ruled in Italy three years and six months, he was slain by the treachery of his wife, and the cause of the murder was this', according to Paulus Deaconus.

While he sat in merriment at a banquet at Verona longer than was proper, with the drinking-cup he had made of the skull of his slaughtered father-in-law, he ordered it to be given to the queen, Rosemund, to drink wine from it, and he invited her merrily to drink with her father. Lest this should seem impossible to anyone, I speak the truth in Christ. I saw King Ratchis [at whose court Paul was educated] holding this cup in his hand on a certain festal day to show it to his guests. Then Rosemund, when she heard the thing, conceived in her heart deep anguish that she could not restrain, and straightway she burned to revenge the death of her father by the murder of her husband.

Rosemund impersonated her own dressing-maid with whom the strong man of the court, Peredeo, 'was accustomed to have intercourse, and then Peredeo, coming in ignorance, lay with the queen. And when the wicked act was already accomplished and she asked him who he thought her to be', Rosemund revealed herself, thereby blackmailing Peredeo. 'Then Rosemund, while Alboin had given himself up to a noon-day sleep, ordered that there should be a great silence in the palace, and taking away all other arms, she bound his sword tightly to the head of the bed so it could not be taken away or unsheathed, and according to Peredeo [by now the adviser rather than the executioner in the matter] she, more cruel than any beast, let in Helemechis the murderer.' Against the man whom Rosemund had chosen to commit the actual deed Alboin defended himself with a footstool, 'but unfortunately alas! this most warlike and very brave man being helpless against his enemy, was slain as if he were one of no account, and he who was most famous in war through the overthrow of so many enemies, perished by the scheme of one little woman'.

The lives of the Lombards were daubed with blood: the least developed of the Germanic barbarian invaders, they pillaged and slaughtered to gain their conquests and then persisted likewise among themselves. If the term 'Dark Ages' means the darkness of slaughter, the darkness of the uncivilized, then the Lombards define it. Rosemund married her co-murderer Helmechis, who tried with her to usurp the kingdom, and when this failed they fled to Ravenna.

Then the prefect Longinus began to urge Rosemund to kill Helmechis and join him, Longinus, in wedlock. As she was ready for every kind of wickedness and as she desired to become mistress of the people of Ravenna, she gave her consent to the accomplishment of this great crime, and while Helmechis was bathing himself, she offered him, as he came out of the bath, a cup of poison which she said was for his health. But when he felt that he had drunk the cup of death, he compelled Rosemund, having drawn his sword upon her, to drink what was left, and thus these most wicked murderers perished at one moment by the judgement of God Almighty.

These ages darken further in terms of the information available. The picture of the Lombard period remains hard to grasp, especially in the flashing darts in which Paul, whose opinions and capacity for factual innovation not infrequently overthrow the historian in him, illuminates the landscape. He begins long passages of early, necessary but obscure history where legend and fact seemed indistinguishable with sentences worthy of a novelist rather than a historian: 'At this time a certain prostitute had brought forth seven little boys at a birth, and the mother, more cruel than all wild beasts, threw them into a fish-pond to be drowned....' Several chapters begin with tantalizing environmental snapshots: 'At this time there was a deluge of water in the territory of Venetia and Liguria, and in other regions of Italy such as is believed not to have existed since the time of Noah. Ruins were made of estates and country seats, and at the same time a great destruction of men and animals. . . .'

Behaviour under pressure also casts fresh, if oblique, light on these untrammelled people. When the Avars over-ran the Lombards in a sharp and vicious war in the region of Venice about a hundred miles due east ahead of me, they impaled the rebellious Lombard queen – Paul calls her 'abominable harlot' – on a stake in the middle of a field. Her daughters, 'striving from love of chastity not to be contaminated by the barbarians . . . put the flesh of raw chickens under the band between their breasts, and this, when putrified by the heat, gave out an evil smell. And the Avars, when they wanted to touch them, could not endure the stench that they thought was natural to them, but moved far away from them with cursing, saying that all the Langobard women had a bad smell.' Paul recommends this stratagem to all women eager for chastity in such circumstances.

Irritating road from Como to Bergamo, especially in the rain. These villages and small towns will soon be joined together as one continuous stringy suburb, peppered with ugly light industry and scabby, straggling smallholdings – unlike the precise farms and manicured allotments with their minuscule wood huts along the railway lines of Switzerland. The thunderstorm in Como last night came straight out of Wagner: long flashes along the lake right upon the huge peals which, as every child knows, means that the storm is raging right overhead. It seemed to travel up and down the lake at will, never leaving and taking off to where it belonged, in the hills and wooded mountains. Beyond Bergamo the hard decision again forced itself upon me – to leave the small roads of the people and take the motorways of the impersonal. It turned out to be the right decision. Only from the *autostrada* could I begin to see the prettiness of the distant villages, the walled small towns which had been obscured by their own local outcrops of buildings as I drove through them.

I stopped for lunch at Desenzano, a village on Lake Garda, twenty miles or so west of Verona. 'Verona further seems than India, Lake Garda is remote as the Red Sea', wrote the fourth-century poet Claudian Claudianus, and so it must have seemed from his beloved, triumphal Rome. Digressions in multiple choices now came dangerously close to irresistibility. For instance, the map reveals a famous and familiar name just off this eastwards route; is it the same place whose name graces the tables of the restaurants even in faraway Rome? In the legends another Irish pilgrim died of thirst on his road to Rome, and where he fell there rose by his head a great inexhaustible mineral spring – which in veneration they called San Pellegrino.

Only six others ate in the restaurant at Desenzano, all Americans, a party of four and an ancient couple who apologized that they could not eat their salad as the waitress had given them too much food. The water lapped hard and direct beneath the window, and the view changed as the mist on the lake came and went with the hydrofoil. When a new corner of the far distance appeared, picked out by a tranche of sun which managed to shaft through the midday gloom, the scene turned into an Edwardian engraving – crags appeared and the village on the far shore, with a small campanile and cream houses, looked like a miniature Venice. Now the light moved to another part of the lake and in a tint of mist and ochre revealed another group of houses much farther away. Hilaire Belloc on his *Path to Rome* observed, 'If one wanted to give a rich child a perfect model or toy, one could not give him anything better than an Italian lake.' The light changed again over the poplars on the little peninsula on the far side and the hydrofoil returned, disturbing the water. The wind had risen further and old people clutched at their summer hats along the *lungo di lago*. My thin green pasta had been heavily infiltrated by garlic; the local wine had the colour of nutty blood. The sun came out again for the umpteenth time revealing distant cypresses and houses behind tall walls, a brusque and confident contrast to the hard-edged, muddy survival, the bad-toothed, ill-clad ekeing endured by the citizens of the Dark Ages.

The light distracts so, even from the exquisite poetry of a local – the Mantuan, Publius Vergilius Maro. A poet's poet: to Cecil Day-Lewis, who translated him, he became 'that divine poet'; Pope called his *Eclogues* 'the sweetest poems in all the world'; Tennyson, 'at the request of the Mantuans for the nineteenth century of Virgil's death', wrote an ode which called him 'lord of language' and described him as the 'light among the vanished ages'. The Irish writer Helen Waddell, who in her own undoubted commitment to Christianity still applauded 'the pagan learning that flows like a sunk river through the mediaeval centruries', summarized Virgil's importance: 'the beacon to guide ages to come, the voice not only of Rome, but of all mankind, the pattern of history, and perhaps the pattern of eternity, translated into time'. Dryden called the *Georgics*, Virgil's four-volume poetic essay, written between 37 and 30 BC during the poet's thirties, 'the best poem of the best poet – he licked his verses into shape as a she-bear her cubs'. His poems praise the countryside, urge the reader to enjoy the fruits of these small hills where he was born:

Here spring is everlasting, and the summer extends into months not its own: the cattle bring forth their young twice a year, the apple tree produces fruit twice. There are no ravening tigers, or fierce brood of lions, no deadly nightshade deceives the unwary pickers, no scaly snakes writhe in immense spirals or coil in mighty sweeps over the ground. Think too of our many lovely cities, the toil of men's efforts, all those towns we have built heaped high on their sheer cliffs and the rivers gliding beneath their ancient walls.

Virgil achieved superstar recognition in his own lifetime, lionized by both plebs and patricians; his verses were found scratched on the walls of Pompeii. He left these parts early, went to Rome and then Campania. His connection with the land continued to fuel him, and even though the heroic/historiographic *Aeneid* became his monument, the boyhood spent on the farm near Mantua permanently illuminated his vision. This road, heading towards Verona and Ferrara and his own Mantua, is still his landscape: the sun flooded it as I drove through, hoping that the monk from the Skelligs had picked up even a snatch of Virgil, perhaps the *Aeneid*.

By 687, though, any traveller would have been much more concerned with the political situation, since his safety depended upon it. At least among the Franks sides had already been taken, and intelligence would have been available as to which kingdom or mayoralty would receive such a traveller favourably. (Wilfrid, for instance, was assured of an uncertain welcome, to say the least, among the Austrasians in eastern Francia, especially having been offered the see of Strasbourg by their upstart, the returning carpetbagger Dagobert.) Here, in these hills and plains, uncertainty rather than unity reigned. The Exarchs of the Eastern Roman Empire, Constantinople's lieutenants, still administered Ravenna – but the Lombards lived nearby. They too lived a little nervously. Shortly after my monk's time a Lombard king promulgated a law requiring all travellers from north of the Alps to carry a passport. The Lombards lived in terror of invasion by the Franks – justifiable terror, as it eventually turned out.

In 687, 119 years had elapsed since Alboin led the Lombards with their luggage into the Po valley. They entered a land which had just experienced a period of enormous and troubled flux. While Rome had been building its Empire, tribal movement downwards from Scandinavia, to escape a climate changing from temperate to harsh, had taken place continuously for five centuries – before, and for a time after, the birth of Christ – and the wanderers settled in eastern Germany. The Goths among them continued to travel, and along the Black Sea in the second century AD they split into roughly two groups, Ostrogoths and Visigoths. From further east came a barbarian people of Mongol derivation, the Huns, who first of all routed the Ostrogoths, and then put pressure on all the peoples who had settled in Germany. Those of western Germany, Angles, Saxons and Franks, migrated westwards, and since they had come of settled, farming stock tended largely to conform to their tribal model. Those of eastern Germany, Burgundians (who became part of emerging Francia), Gepids and those who defeated them, the Lombards, Goths and Vandals, continued, like their herdsmen ancestors, to roam.

All – in due course – exerted pressure on the Roman Empire. In order to escape the Huns the Visigoths crossed the Danube in 376, at first with the agreement of the Emperor Valens, whom they had petitioned; then they defeated him at the battle of Adrianople in 378. 'By the care of his attendants', wrote Edward Gibbon,

Valens was removed from the field of battle to a neighbouring cottage, where they attempted to dress his wound and to provide for his future safety. But this humble retreat was instantly surrounded by the enemy; they tried to force the door; they were provoked by a discharge of arrows from the roof; till at length, impatient of delay, they set fire to a pile of dry faggots, and consumed the cottage with the Roman emperor and his train.

Adrianople was the most crushing defeat the Romans had suffered in almost six hundred years. It taught them that the old Roman infantry legions were obsolete – from now on Germanic cavalry were to dominate the army – and led increasingly to the policy of buying off the barbarian invaders that was eventually to procure the downfall of the Western Empire.

In 410 Alaric the Goth – whose earlier invasion from the east had so shaken the Empire that 'even the legion which had been stationed to guard the wall of Britain against the Caledonians of the North was hastily recalled' – actually besieged and brought to her knees 'the queen of the world', the brilliant city of Rome itself. 'Many thousands of the inhabitants of Rome expired in their houses, or in the streets, for want of sustenance; and as the public sepulchres without the walls were in the power of the enemy' – how Gibbon enjoyed lurid moments – 'the stench which arose from so many putrid and unburied carcasses infected the air; and the miseries of famine were succeeded and aggravated by the contagion of a pestilential disease.'

These two events, Adrianople and Alaric's onslaught on Rome, stand out like giant markers on the downward path of the Empire, which the invaders began to dismantle. Increasingly throughout the fifth century, and especially after the death of Attila in 453, those Germanic tribes who had been under constant pressure from Attila's Huns emerged as forces in their own right. Since they no longer had to fight Attila they could now afford to flex their muscles in other directions of their own choosing. The Angles and Saxons began to expand forcibly in Britain. The Franks took control of northern Gaul, with the Burgundians a considerable presence in Alpine and Rhône territories. The Vandals crossed the Rhine in 406 and went on to rupture the Empire's demeanour in North Africa. By 455 they commanded the North African shore of the western Mediterranean and sailed up the Tiber with their well-fed fleet to attack Rome. The Visigoths had penetrated as far as south-west France and had established considerable power in Spain.

The Empire which they were all attacking had substantially changed its complexion from the traditional Rome-based institution of the early Caesars. Rome still remained an emblem, and attacks upon it still constituted havoc, but the administration was conducted from elsewhere. In 325, nineteen years after his soldiers had hailed him 'Caesar' at York, Constantine embarked upon becoming 'the Great'. He assessed his wide Empire shrewdly, reasoned that Rome's effectiveness as a central post of command had diminished. It was no longer a swift, convenient supply and power base to defend borders as far-flung and diverse as Persia, the Rivers Danube and Rhine, Gaul, Britain, Spain, Syria and Africa. The Empire needed two imperial centres, East and West. In the East he chose a fishing town called Byzantium. In the West – though Rome still played a part – Milan evolved as the Empire's headquarters. When Alaric attacked Milan, the Western Emperor Honorius, young and fearful, moved his headquarters in 403. According to Gibbon,

The recent danger to which the person of the emperor had been exposed in the defenceless palace of Milan urged him to seek a retreat in some inaccessible fortress of Italy where he might securely remain, while the open country was covered by a deluge of barbarians. On the coast of the Hadriatic, about ten or twelve miles from the most southern of the seven mouths of the Po, the Thessalians had founded the ancient colony of Ravenna, which they afterwards resigned to the natives of Umbria. The adjacent country, to the distance of many miles, was a deep and impassable morass; and the artificial causeway which connected Ravenna with the continent might be easily guarded or destroyed on the approach of an hostile army.

It was in Ravenna that Caesar had prepared his troops for the crossing of the Rubicon, four and a half centuries before.

For seven years Honorius had the powerful assistance of his mentor, the general Flavius Stilicho, himself a Vandal, who contained Alaric and even defeated him when he tried to take Verona. As a result of what Gibbon calls 'the obscure intrigues of the palace of Ravenna' – it was whispered that he was too soft on his fellow Vandals – Stilicho fell from favour with the Emperor: 'the respectful attachment of Honorius was converted into fear, suspicion and hatred', and Stilicho was beheaded in Ravenna in 408. Honorius, ever more beleaguered, unable to rule effectively without the strength of his trusted senior adviser, died of dropsy in 423.

In 476 Odovacar or Odoacer, a German officer of barbarian descent, raised an army which deposed the Western Emperor, Romulus – at which point Odovacar suggested to the senate that the Western Empire did not now require an emperor. He therefore chose to rule himself, and the moment of his assumption is pointed to in history's shorthand as the moment at which the Western Roman Empire ceased to exist. 'Odoacer', says Gibbon, 'was the first barbarian who reigned in Italy, over a people who had once asserted their just superiority above the rest of mankind. The disgrace of the Romans still excites our respectful compassion, and we fondly sympathise with the imaginary grief and indignation of their degenerate posterity.'

Odovacar did not rule well: during his reign 'the country was exhausted by the irretrievable losses of war, famine and pestilence. . . . After a reign of fourteen years Odoacer was oppressed by the superior genius of Theodoric, king of the Ostrogoths; a hero alike excellent in the arts of war and of government, who restored an age of peace and prosperity, and whose name still excites and deserves the attention of mankind' – and whose presence can still be felt, I am told, in the gleaming town ahead of me, Ravenna.

On a sunlit Saturday afternoon, past those distant brown villages which threaten to spill down the side of their hills, I arrived in the only town I have ever wanted to steal, the beautiful cobbled place that claims Virgil. I prefer the town's Italian name, Mantova. Round a bend in the road a dome appeared, some spires, that terracotta again, cinnamon impressions, then a bridge, then a lagoon from which the light rose brightly.

Until this point in his journey the Dark Ages traveller from Ireland had seen little enough in stone, and then not well-built: the White House of Ninian in Galloway, occasional Roman ruins across Britain, a monastery or two in Ireland or England, overgrown villas of Gallo-Roman luminaries in France, a Merovingian palace rising above the wood and wattle houses of Reims, but nothing which prepared him for the extent and richness of the architecture of the south, of the Adriatic and then the Mediterranean. Mantova began to fill that void.

The Cathedral in Mantova has a self-possessed air which it has had for several centuries, due to a relic entrusted into its care. When Jesus Christ died on the cross a Roman officer ascertained death with a spear, causing one of the famous wounds of the stigmata, the condition which some devout people believe they may have inherited. In their bodies appear the replications of the wounds of Christ – the hands, the feet and the long wound in the side caused by the spear of Longinus.

Not long after Good Friday the centurion converted to Christianity, so moved did he feel by the events of the Crucifixion, and he had within his possession the blood he had gathered at that consummate moment on Calvary. Longinus took his place in the general hagiographical development of Christianity within the first six centuries or so; he became 'the good Roman'. The blood he collected, which also entered the Holy Grail legends, came to Mantova, was enshrined within what became the Cathedral and annually forms the centre of religious veneration.

The Cathedral at Mantova has been undergoing restoration, and despite the beautiful and monumental coolness does not offer the same opportunities for contemplation as it otherwise might. Outside, the colonnades of the palaces and their courtyards do not urbanize the place so much that you forget the rhythms of the surrounding countryside, the small hills, the light off much water. In the streets, grass sprouts from the less busy cobbles, and a canal, with fronds and moss at the water's edge, slips between the terracotta alleyways, beneath the sloping roofs with their crazy ginger-bread tilts. Those who built this exquisite town and who commissioned the wall paintings and large frescoes with a cast of local people – heavy faces, brooding and watchful, swarthy-lidded eyes, rich fabrics in gold and red and black, modest but wealthy head-dresses on the gentlewomen of the court – gave their gift to the world long after 687. However, the power of towns such as Mantova derives from the political upheavals of that time, when the history of Italy changed yet again within a century or so, and the foundations of a disunited state were laid by the Lombards a century after Theodoric the Ostrogoth.

Theodoric, son of an Ostrogothic king settled in the Danube valley, was enabled to overthrow Odovacar because the Emperor Zeno in Constantinople both hated Odovacar's domination in Italy and feared Theodoric's growing military power, which could be turned against Constantinople. Zeno achieved the by now typical Roman compromise – he turned both his greatest threats inwards upon each other. He promised that if Odovacar could be defeated Theodoric could rule Italy. In 493, after a campaign which lasted almost five years, Theodoric won, and at a treacherous banquet in Ravenna murdered Odovacar. Theodoric then governed Italy, outwardly in the name of the Roman Emperor, though when he had coins struck bearing the Emperor's head he had his own likeness or initials placed on the obverse. Although he gave himself the title of *Rex* – taking care not to stipulate the precise jurisdiction of his kingdom – and although he wore the purple robes exclusive to an emperor, Theodoric did not publicly overstep the imperial boundaries in a way that the Emperor in Constantinople would have found provocative or intolerable. He attempted to rule well, in a more civilized fashion than might have been expected from a 'barbarian' – he had after all been educated for a decade in Constantinople and was a Christian, though of the Arian heresy, like most of the Goths.

In the beginning his reign achieved widespread popularity by harnessing Roman thought and skill to the energy and drive of the Goths. He embarked upon a building programme to restore the towns and morale of Italy, both of which had been crumbling, and he attempted remarkable legal unification – 'one law and equal discipline' for Romans and Goths. He shrewdly had in his entourage Flavius Magnus Aurélius Cassiodorus, a Calabrian whom he appointed as his secretary and mouthpiece. Cassiodorus was able to promulgate the thoughts of his master in an enhancing way. 'Understand', Cassiodorus reported Theodoric as declaring, 'that men progress not so much by bodily violence as by reason, and that those who deserve the greatest praise are those who excel others in justice.' Such statements – particularly in a culture which had, in its 'barbarian' incarnation, glorified violent action and disconsidered intellect – amounted to revolution. It meant that by the late seventh century, when the Irish monk walked through, at least one barbarian kingdom had some experience of trying to apply the mind instead of the sword, an uncommon experiment among those tribes which had invaded from Germany.

In fact, the level of thought which Theodoric tried to bring to bear upon the governance of Italy – he attempted, initially at least, to create a one-nation, post-barbarian state – would seem remarkable even if it had not been established in the brutal and turbulent context of the times. As well as Cassiodorus, he had another great official who made an equally powerful contribution to his social and policy ambitions – Anicius Manlius Torquatus Severinus Boethius, who had spent eighteen years in the academies of Athens attempting, as Gibbon suggests, 'to reconcile the strong and subtle sense of Aristotle with the devout contemplation and sublime fancy of Plato'.

Boethius had contemplated 'the geometry of Euclid, the music of Pythagoras, the arithmetic of Nichomachus, the mechanics of Archimedes, the astronomy of Ptolemy and the logic of Aristotle ... and he alone was esteemed capable of describing the wonders of art, a sundial, a water-clock, or a sphere which represented the motions of the planets'. He then devoted himself to public service, in which his fine mind and eloquent voice were 'uniformly exerted in the cause of innocence and humanity'. He became a consul in 510, but times had not become so civilized that he did not fall foul of his king. He was condemned for alleged treason and 'magic', wrote in gaol five volumes *On the Consolation of Philosophy*, was tortured – a cord was tied around his head 'and forcibly tightened till his eyes almost started from their sockets' – and was beaten to death in 524. Later he was canonized as St Severinus and his Latin paraphrases of the Greek philosophers became the sole source of Greek thought in the Middle Ages. Cassiodorus (perhaps through prudence) fared more fortunately and retired to a monastery which he founded.

Theodoric's reign, more ambitious than successful, created divisions and eventually became riven with typical suspicions. Boethius and Cassiodorus had tried to persuade their master to introduce laws which moved government continually towards the principle of equality. He did not, however, succeed in uniting Romans and Goths: complex legal divisions remained in which both factions obeyed laws held in common but administered by separate Roman and Gothic judiciaries. The army was exclusively Gothic, and Romans were forbidden to bear arms. Religious division played a part too. Those Goths who had been Christianized had embraced Arianism, a belief originated by an Egyptian priest called Arius who, in the fourth century, argued that since Christ was the Son of God he was therefore junior to God and therefore less than God. Furthermore, since Christ had a stated birth he did not possess the necessary quality of eternity, as the whole True God had no beginning and no end. The matter appeared to be resolved at the Council called by Constantine at Nicea in 325, which declared Christ, in the Nicene Creed, 'God from God, Light from Light, True God from True God, begotten not made' – therefore to true Christians 'one in substance with the Father'. In theory that declaration settled the question: in practice entire peoples, such as Theodoric's Ostrogoths, retained the Arian beliefs. Theodoric, though he did not contest the Catholicism of the Romans, built churches in which to worship in the Arian creed, further emphasizing the divisions he had hoped to heal.

Finally, after some years of considerable unease between Theodoric and the papacy, and between Theodoric and Constantinople, where the Emperor was persecuting those who remained Arians, Theodoric ordered, on 30 August 526, that all Catholic churches in Italy should be assigned to the Arians. He died, though, on the very day he made the decree.

From Mantova I took the road to Ferrara, a different town altogether, more fortified, more self-conscious, higher and not as humble. The road between the two wanders contiguous to the Po. Across the meadows beyond Ferrara, standing by the river, the warm terracotta towers of village churches appear, like local jewellery – satellites to the place which has been called 'the most interesting town in Italy', some say 'in Europe'. Ravenna overwhelms, overstimulates, and the pleasure redoubled for me in the certain knowledge that the glories on display certainly bathed the eye of any seventh-century travelling monk – the basilica of San Vitale had, after all, been consecrated on 17 May 548.

Honorius abandoned Milan for Ravenna in 403 – I have placed the monk from the Skelligs on the streets of Ravenna in 687. In those two and three-quarter centuries, the fortunes of the city swung from Roman to Gothic and back again. Theodoric, in Gibbon's words, 'preferred the residence of Ravenna, where he cultivated an orchard with his own hands'. His tomb there is one of the treasures of the place. During the years that followed his death, years in which Ravenna was still in the power of Theodoric's successors, Justinian (of whom more later) began his huge campaign to recover the lost ground of the old Roman Empire. In 539 Belisarius, Justinian's brilliant general, captured Ravenna and accepted the Goths' surrender. Justinian, and after him successive emperors in Constantinople, appointed exarchs to rule Ravenna, and while the Byzantine Empire retained its swathe across Italy Ravenna remained a keystone city, though

The Basilica of San Vitale, Ravenna.

hemmed in north and south, if not westward. The exarchs were in office, therefore, in 687, with directions to answer unambiguously to the Emperor in Constantinople. This remained the position – despite some local insurrection – until the Lombards under King Liutprand captured the city in 727, marking the beginning of the end of Ravenna's Byzantine commitment.

The glories to be seen in Ravenna today were created over a long period – from the earliest days before Honorius to the high point of Justinian's triumphal Empire. As you look up from street corners, the high skies give a hint of the broad lakelands and the Adriatic. Within walking distance of the Piazza del Popolo the compact town holds great treasures – churches, tombs, baptisteries, of which at least five or six stand as greater or smaller wonders of the world, a status attributable wholly to Ravenna's mosaicists. It is wondrous that so much technical expertise and colour could have been available as early as the fifth and sixth centuries: marvellous, too, that patrons existed with sufficient perception to commission the work, even if vanity may have been one of their motives.

Honorius's death in 410 placed his sister, Augusta Galla Placidia, in eventual command. Captured when the Goths sacked Rome and forced into marriage with a Gothic chieftain, she was restored to her stature in Italy in 416. Now widowed, she fled Ravenna to escape an incestuously inclined, dropsical brother. Her uncle in Constantinople, Theodosius, the Emperor of the East, gave her shelter and then restored her to Ravenna. Here she acted as a protector for a quarter of a century, and during this period the mosaic artists flourished in this ancient town. One of the earliest buildings in Ravenna commemorates the name and memory of Galla Placidia. She died in 450, in Rome it is thought, but in her lifetime a mausoleum was built in Ravenna which followed that spiritual theme of the ideal relationship between the body and the soul – a plain building outside, with the interior most beautifully decorated, in this case with mosaics.

Not a large building – not quite forty-two feet long, and thirty-three and a half feet wide; twenty people would fill it beyond comfort, though the arched roof offers breathing space. Two hundred lire in the meter outside give light, and the mosaics are revealed. The cupola of the mausoleum has been schemed as a starry sky, the floor of Heaven. A quartet of figures commands the base of the dome – a man, an ox, a lion and an eagle, the symbols of Matthew, Luke, Mark and John, each resting upon, or rising from, a whisper of red and white cloud. The roof of the entrance to this cruciform building has the traditional shape of a barrel, and it consists of one continuous mass of gold and white flower-stars, crystal-snowflaked on a background of the blue sky of early night. Not a square inch has been left unadorned. The mosaicists covered all the surfaces in a profusion of reds and blues and yellows and greens and browns and whites – primary colours and rainbows and many, many shades and hues, brilliant as well as subtle.

The Good Shepherd in gold robe with blue stripe sits among his sheep, wearing thonged sandals, on a small outcrop of gold-tinged rock, with fern and palm: the sheep have fat tails. Bronze deer lower their antlers through friendly undergrowth, pairs of doves drink from bowls or contemplate a small fountain. Peter and Paul, the Lamb of God, flowers, fruits, birds, crosses, shrubs and abstract forms greet every turn of the head. One continuous basket of flowers arches right across the barrel shape where the entrance becomes the centre of the building, while another arch of a long, geometric frieze reaches the same distance – and all in colours that might have been mixed yesterday.

Some stone sarcophagi stand on the floor. Even though the mausoleum has been named after Augusta Galla Placidia, the folklore and the history agree that she may have been buried in Rome. This building immortalizes her protectorate and her patronage, and the brilliant interior has the same smell as the beehive huts on Skellig Michael, a dusty smell of stone. Not many other comparisons have validity – even though the mosaics in the mausoleum also honour the Christian tradition, with no hint of the Eastern influence that was to come from Byzantium. Skellig Michael did not, it would appear, get a monastery for at least a century after these buildings were consecrated. The two places shared the same tradition, of a Christian imagery and canon, the leadership of Peter, the intellect of Paul, the iconography of the Lamb of God and the Good Shepherd, the doves, the fountains, the scriptures and the echoes of the natural world. So that if a wandering scholar from Ireland marvelled at these images he none the less connected with them and received them, regardless of Arianism or Whitby or any of the other intellectual difficulties which shivered through the early Church.

Across the courtyard from the mausoleum stands Ravenna's showpiece, the basilica of San Vitale. Built a century after the mausoleum, it bore the name of a gentleman of Bologna, Vitale, who took instruction in Christianity from his slave – both received the honour of martyrdom. To an even greater degree it commemorates Justinian, then at the height of his success. The basilica, made of thin russet bricks on layers of lime mortar, has an air of strength and calm, bulking large and multi-layered, on levels of fat, short towers, angled roofs of curved tiles. At the core rises a high octagonal central building, and a bell-tower stands a little away and higher than the rest. The arched windows harmonize in shape with the main door, and the stepped levels give an impression of bulky security whose peaceful mood comes from the colours of the brick and the lime mortar. Work began in 527 and finished in 548. The mosaics of the interior were designed to be included as part of the architecture.

Such range and accomplishment, technical and thematic: Moses receiving the Ten Commandments on Mount Sinai, with the angels announcing

Carved stone capital from San Vitale, Ravenna.

the birth of Isaac to Abraham, while Sarah stands by the door, smiling, a finger held to her lips in a shushing surprise for her husband; wreaths of flowers, leaves and fruit, pears, apples, soft fruits, with the fantails of the quartet of peacocks symbolizing the Resurrection; the bread and wine sacrifice of Melchizedek and, opposite him, across the white-and-gold-clothed altar, Abel, holding a lamb aloft in offering; Moses approaching the burning trees; Abraham preparing to sacrifice his beloved son Isaac; St Vitale receiving the crown of martyrdom; the Emperor Justinian walking with a frown to his place of worship, accompanied by equally concerned priests and alert soldiers bearing shields and spears.

Under billowing canopies of blue and red, along a green lawn, the Empress Theodora leads a stunning procession of women, all of whom have aware expressions, and by a fountain they prepare to enter a portal under a raised curtain; they wear jewels and robes falling in folds, and their faces have seen pleasure. Angels surround and support Christ, hawks and ravens strive to keep their balance, trees grow tall and bushy and green beside the walls of Bethlehem and Jerusalem, which have been studded with green jewels. The birds of the air and the beasts of the field, heron, ibis, dove, tortoise, lamb, terrifying lion, confident ox – all appear, composed and immortalized in these tiny squares, *tesserae*, of stone, glass, serpentine, marble. The dull red brooch which the Emperor Justinian wears to fasten his cloak on the right shoulder is in fact a large, fashioned chip of cornelian.

In small dark corners, beneath the breathing of the eight high arches and their noble columns, the treasures continue, and in the broad weaves of the mosaics each glance divulges something new, some fresh detail, with a gasp of charm, some small nudge of sheer joy – like the tortoise slogging his way towards the legs of the stork, or the anger on the face of the lion or the smile of Abraham's wife. San Vitale amounts to a gift – of a different world, created by highly skilled workmen, who worked long hot hours, exempt from taxes, and all paid for by a sixth-century banker who lived nearby and who called every day to see how his munificence progressed. Virgil, in book four of the *Aeneid*, recalls Iris, the unsleeping goddess whose persona dwelt in the rainbow, down which she glided with her messages from Zeus: in the context of the mosaics the description fits Ravenna, the last capital that the Roman and Byzantine Empires had in the West:

> Downward the various goddess took her flight
> And drew a thousand colours from the light.

Blinking in the sunlight outside the basilica, but still within the embrace of San Vitale, you will see the Museo Nazionale, which, housed in a wing of the former Benedictine monastery, has a vast display. Even by taking account only of those exhibits which, in terms of their period, fit the purposes of my (that is to say, the monk's) journey, it would still be impossible to consider all within a week – or, with any thought, a year.

Begin with finds consistent with Celtic burial rites, Iron Age weapons, bronze clasps and fasteners – they could have come from the museum in Dublin or the one on the Rock of Cashel, with the Hallstatt sword and the gorgets. A monastery might have found them and kept them either as curios or in its own small collection, gathered out of antiquarian interest for the wonder and education of the monks, for the visual benefit of the *scriptorium*.

Progress to the Hermaphrodite Room: among many fifth- and sixth-century images it contains the sculpture of Hercules capturing the Hind of Ceryneia, a year-long Labour to bring back this wonderful creature with her hooves of bronze and horns of gold. Other rooms display textiles and tunics from the seventh century, which the Irish monk would have seen on the people in the streets and markets of Ravenna (some walking along with eucalyptus leaves held to their noses to abate odours); lead pipes bearing the Emperor's name, still in use then – one of Theodoric's reforms aimed to restore the water supplies in towns where the pipes had become dilapidated or overgrown; the carved covers of books, secular and religious, in use in Ravenna during the seventh century – a visiting monk, a guest or assistant at worship, could have handled these; a green wine jug, or a violet one, a cloudy drinking cup with a rim of raised indigo glass as a grip running lazily around the circumference; gold coins, used as payment to the artists who decorated San Vitale.

A corner of the museum belongs to the early Benedictine cloister. The shaded rooms off the cloister contain the shards and jigsawed restorations of *amphorae* and terracotta vessels. Where the grass in the cloister square grows long, burnt and untended various monumental fragments line the walls of the paved walks. They include stones bearing Roman inscriptions; representations of the Lamb of God; chunks of sarcophagi; wistful images of children taken from first-century tombs; a carpenter's gravestone which shows him using an adze. One tall stone the colour of oatmeal has an image which recurred on this journey and in circumstances far away from that hot dusty morning by the salt-marshes of the Adriatic – the cross with extremities like the letter T carved in the rock at Ninian's Cave on the west coast of Scotland, and which appeared again in a glass-fronted museum showcase in Toul.

The other treasures of Ravenna take days to inspect. The basilica of Sant'

Apollinare Nuovo, whose high, cylindrical bell-tower led some scholars to believe that the architecture of Ravenna had caused or influenced the Irish Round Towers, has long marching friezes of mosaics as brilliant as those of San Vitale. Magi, a procession of virgins, apostles, a series of miracles – including the raising of Lazarus, portrayed as a white mummy staggering from the tomb – angels, Pilate washing his hands and the Last Supper, martyrs, harbour walls made of wide bricks, square-rigged ships in the port,

Sant' Apollinare Nuovo, Ravenna.

doves, stars and ferns – all gleam on a gold background. They run the length of this peaceful, three-naved, colonnaded building with twelve columns on either side of the main nave. The octagonal Arian Baptistery shows a naked Christ, standing waist-high in transparent water, being baptized by John the Baptist. The image recurs in the Neonian Baptistery, behind the Cathedral by the Piazza del Duomo; this building, also octagonal, erected around 380, predates both San Vitale and the Mausoleum of Galla Placidia. The mosaics here have, if anything, a greater intensity than in the other buildings, as if the artists crammed in everything they thought of, lest they might never have such good ideas again – swirling festoons of acanthus leaves, bordered with broad stripes of red and green, inhabited by apostles in gold or white tunics, altars, peacocks, icons and crosses.

The fifth-century basilica of St John the Evangelist, built by Augusta Galla Placidia in thanksgiving for being saved from shipwreck on her return to Ravenna, has no elaborate mosaics of the period: a later abbot removed them all in the fashionable interests of renewed austerity. The fifth-century basilica of St Francis has a flooded crypt through whose clear waters tantalizing fragments of mosaic appear. The sixth-century church of St Agatha, small, pretty, often overlooked, has mosaics of leaves and roundels, broken and dispersed in earthquakes and wars.

At the edge of the town Theodoric's Mausoleum, a powerhouse of cut stone, has the same T cross of Whithorn, this time housed in a circle, unlike that in the museum cloister and therefore more reminiscent of Ninian's marigold cross, though not as free and arciform. The tomb was built on the orders of the King in 520. They roofed it with a single vaulted block of stone, 108 feet in circumference and weighing 300 tons, quarried on the Istrian peninsula across the gulf of Venice and brought south-westwards on a specially built raft to Ravenna. A split in the stone prompts the legend of Theodoric's sudden death. Lightning struck him while he stood within the mausoleum – revenge, they said, for his ordering the surrender of all the Catholic churches in Italy, that very day, to his own Arian co-religionists. Variations on the legend say he fell off his horse during a thunderstorm, was swallowed by a volcano on whose crater's rim he stood, or died of a seizure after he cut open a fish he was about to eat and found the head of an enemy within. His 'palace' stands on the Via di Roma, a much-altered and later building, constructed, it is suggested, on the site of the earlier imperial residence where Theodoric grew his orchard.

The energy which Ravenna once had may still be seen. It lies within the long marching friezes of apostles, virgins, martyrs, lords and ladies on the immediacy of that gold background, and the peacocks and the doves by the little fountains. It parades among the geometric borders in red, green, blue, gold and indigo. It inhabits the animals and the sacrifices and the jewelled walls of Bethlehem, and that extraordinary fan-splay of colour in blue, gold, red and yellow by a window opening in San Vitale, so savagely uncompromising in its execution, so restful in its achievement.

Ravenna confirmed an observation made by Samuel Butler in *Erewhon*: 'Time walks beside us and flings back shutters as we advance; but the light thus given often dazzles us, and deepens the darkness which is in front.' Theodoric has been blamed by some historians for ushering in the Dark Ages in Italy by attempting to implement a cultural reformation which he misunderstood and finally misplaced, thereby causing confusion and eventual regression where he wished for progress. Whether or not the allegation seems unfair, the truth of the Ages' Darkness lay ahead of me. Between Ravenna and Rome lay many beautiful places, lands strewn with walled towns in terrain to which many travellers have lost their hearts. Useless to me, though – their eminence did not bud until long after the seventh century. The road ahead coiled unflichingly towards Rome, then to the south and finally to Constantinople – irresistible to a traveller who had seen Ravenna and therefore had tasted Byzantium.

The early medieval history of the regions between Ravenna and Rome remains largely obscure. The pleasures of drifting through Tuscany again – the hot days and warm nights, and the vines and the sun on the honey-coloured rocks, the lizards and the cypresses and the fragments of Roman ruins in the long grass off the main roads – did not include a detailed record of how the people lived. The local history of the period never, so far as seems known, got written down, and the national record did not fare much better.

During the sixth century Justinian's desire that all Italy should be liberated from Gothic rule had clearly been misfounded. The 'barbarians' from whom he sought to 'release' Roman citizens formed an integral – and integrated – part of the society, politics and administration of Justinian's Empire, both East and West. Theodoric's efforts to unite the peoples of Italy had not been entirely without effect, and had clear practical developments. Generations of Germanic soldiers had served and went on serving in the Roman Empire and in its Byzantine continuation. This fact involved Germanic officers and men in the regaining of lost imperial provinces – but from Germanic tribes. In other words two lots of German-descended armies fought each other, one to retain, the other to regain slices of the Roman Empire.

For example, when Justinian's successful general, the Armenian eunuch Narses, campaigned against the Goths, he raised an army of 5200 soldiers from among a Germanic tribe, the Lombards (he also had 3000 Huns and several thousand Persians.) On 15 June 552, Narses left Ravenna and after a short and unstoppable sortie south along the coast marched south-west along one of the major Roman roads, the Via Flaminia which ended at Rimini. After raising some local soldiery he set out to engage with Totila, the rampagingly successful Gothic king. In the battle which followed at Tagina, near the modern town of Nocera, just east of Perugia and Assisi,

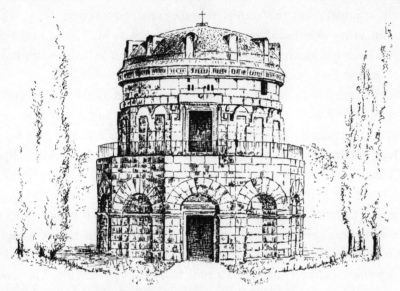

The Mausoleum of Theodoric, Ravenna.

Totila was killed – despite his display of chased gold armour, purple banner and lance-slinging comparable to that of a drum major. In victory the Lombards behaved savagely. They raped the women and girls, often on the altars of the churches, and had to be sent home – whither they marched in triumph – not so much for their atrocious behaviour as for the fact that they had emerged as a force to be feared and Narses wanted to be rid of them.

Fourteen years later, in 566, large areas of Italy, especially in the north, suffered what Paul the Deacon calls 'a very great pestilence ... there began to appear in the groins of men and other rather delicate places a swelling of the glands, after the manner of a nut or a date, presently followed by an unbearable fever, so that upon the third day the man died'. It cleared the landscape, as people fled from it or died where they stood. It emptied the villas and the towns; corpses lay where they fell, their relatives so weak that the effort and infection of any funeral rites proved fatal. 'You might see the world brought back to its ancient silence', wrote Paul, 'no voice in the field, no whistling of shepherds, no lying in wait of wild beasts among the cattle, no harm to domestic fowls. The crops, outliving the time of the harvest, awaited the reaper untouched; the vineyard with its fallen leaves and its shining grapes remained undisturbed while winter came on.' In its disturbed imagination the surviving fragmentary populace heard the muffled blaze of ghostly trumpets and the tramp of thousands of marching feet, as if a phantom army was marching across these very fields I now saw being sprayed by huge machines to keep the crops green and the earth moist. Every village that stood here then became its own mausoleum.

On the night of 14 November 565, Justinian died at the age of eighty-three; the old man's last words appointed his nephew Justin as his successor, and in the morning the new Emperor of Constantinople and his wife Sophia received the applause of the people. The eunuch Narses, who had eclipsed the Goths' power in Italy, had lost his great admirer, and in the next couple of years the envious took over. They whispered against him, pointed to the size of the treasury he had accumulated, noted how well he had done out of his victories. The jealous words reached the ambitious Empress Sophia, who let Narses know that she felt he should be in the palace, in a eunuch's rightful place, carding the thread for the handmaidens' sewing. The piqued Narses has been accused by history of then inviting the Lombards, whose ferocity he had remembered from the battle against Totila, to leave the Hungarian Plain and come to Italy – hence Alboin's arrival in 568 with a huge auxiliary force of Saxon allies. On the heights of Monte Maggiore or Matajur, fifteen miles north of the modern town of Cividale, directly inland from the Gulf of Trieste, the Lombards stood and gazed down into wealthy Italy. Here, the animals grew so large that fifteen men could lie on the hide of one wild ox. The Gothic wars, the plague and resultant famine had debilitated the people. The Lombards, with their long, plaited hair and their pale complexions now red with sunburn and their total lack of niceties, met little enough resistance, and any spirit shown by the Italians was crushed with speed.

The Lombards became a major influence in Italy. They ranged as far as Sicily and even though they never – due to their own disunity – established a single Lombard jurisdiction over the entire country, they commanded large tracts, especially in the north where they first arrived. Later they created individual duchies, such as Spoleto and Beneventum, which became powerfully independent of that original, establishing Lombard kingship. In the year 600, the Lombards ruled all of Italy from the Gulf of Trieste right around the southern edges of the Alps to the Mediterranean and almost as far as Rome. Ravenna, Perugia and Rome stayed in the hands of the exarchs of the Eastern Empire, a thick tranche weaving from the Adriatic to the Mediterranean and sandwiched on the southern side by the Lombard dukes of Spoleto and Beneventum, while Naples and the heel and toe of Italy remained imperial.

The monk's route took him down through the middle of the lands governed by the Exarch of Ravenna. To the north and south lay Lombard dominions. I travelled likewise diagonally across the vertebrae of Italy. In the forest at Caprese, 'the place of the goats', they have restored the house of Michelangelo's birth. (An accidental occurrence: his mother's carriage overturned in a lightning storm and the young Buonarroti arrived a little early.) These areas through which I passed, which came to their full stature in the Renaissance period – towns like Sansepolcro, Anghiari, Città di Castello, which was once levelled by Totila – had in their seventh-century antecedents monks who also acted as local government officials and made returns to Ravenna for the greater government of the Empire. The Church in those days had begun to play an increasing role in the affairs of state: Justinian's Pragmatic Sanction of 554 and his great commissioned Corpus of Civil Law restructured the administration and involved local bishops in the appointments of magistrates and other officials, as well as passing responsibility for such civic details as weights and measures to local priests.

I lost count of the number of times I crossed the Tiber. Maps give a poor impression of how seductive the river becomes as it wanders by Perugia in Umbria and snakes fatly down to Rome. Perugia's domination of the countryside persists: it was taken by Totila, and the later Perugians dug catacombs into the rock beneath their town and used them as siege bases in the many wars against their neighbours. Now the Italians have installed startlingly congruous escalators in these honeycombs to take visitors up into the part of the town where cars are not allowed.

The nights were hot down here, full of mosquitoes from the banks of the

Tiber, assisted by another fly, long-legged and buzzing. In me they found a banquet and feasted night after night. The owner of one small hotel in Narni raised a sympathetic eyebrow when I asked for a mosquito net. He suggested that the bedroom's metal shutters should be kept closed – which seemed illogical, since he advertises the wonderful view down into the old town from the high points along the river, and in any case the heat of the night required wide-open windows. Did they not drain the swamps around here in the early Middle Ages because the mosquitoes killed off appreciably large segments of the local population?

The smallholders still use oxen to pull the plough here. The river appeared again – in the fields off the main roads, through the single streets of dusty yellowed villages that do not even appear on the map, in the acres of tillage divided by raised pipes running like cords across the country. Whether at that moment the stream deserved to be called the Tiber did not matter – it became broader, capable of being followed vaguely down to the outskirts of Rome.

The sacred killing grounds of the Christians, the bloody theatres of the gladiators, the *ad limina* visiting place of the bishops, the consistories of the cardinals, the black smoke, the white smoke, the cry of '*Habemus Papam*', the seminaries of the Irish, the city as Fellini's raddled landscape, the mother-whore of Moravia's writings – a quarter of a million books have been written concerning Rome. When Rome falls the world will end, said Byron: in the 1920s, James Joyce said Rome reminded him of a man 'who lives by exhibiting to travellers his grandmother's corpse'. By 687 Rome had fallen a long way down: even by then it was a city of ruins.

In the fifth and early sixth centuries, while Theodoric ruled, enough of Rome's Caesarean grandeur remained to justify the description of a city, having twenty-four Catholic (as distinct from Arian) churches dedicated to the apostles, two basilicas, over three hundred streets, two Capitols, eighty golden and sixty-four ivory statues of gods, bakeries, reservoirs of clean water, food supply depots, theatres, baths, brothels, a full infrastructure of maintenance, police and tax officials, servicing over 46,000 'ordinary'

The shrine at Delphi: the pillars formed part of the massive temple,
outside which stood a statue of Apollo seventy feet high.

St Benedict: a thirteenth-century representation of the sixth-
century powerhouse who reformed monasticism and created
universal principles of religious community life.

Mohammed taming a lion: a sixteenth-century depiction. Such
miraculous control over wild beasts was also ascribed to Christian
holy men such as Columbanus and Gallus. The prophet is shown
veiled, a convention preferred by many artists.

In the seventh century tribal invaders from the north, Bulgars,
Avars and Slavs, added to Islamic pressures on the Byzantine
Empire from the east. Eleventh-century depictions of events from
these turbulent times.

ρομε να αποσυπιι μετα τουτρακων και μακεδονων καταπο δε ξιου μερος ανιζομενον· κρα
τει μπτους χερσιν και πολιφοουε εργαζεθαι πους αρακηνους· κατα βατρου δε· τον προκο
πιον ανιπαλομενον μετα τους κλαυηκων και ρυπικων· υποπουν εμαν πους τε ζεθαι· ωι
πεμφθει σε δε παρα τους σρατηγου μονπειαο πους απο ρωτι δια τηνμπορη σαμενιηνφιλονει κι
αν· εκλινε πρους πρου πην το κατα τον προκοπιον μερος· και απος εκεινος απεσφαλη τους οι
κοσιπαιγορι σαμενος· και καιλωπουτ πον μαχυρα πεσσαιν·

δε λεεων· Α λοντ και επρου απερ γαζαθαι λαμπρον· και το εκ τυσε ριδος συκιασι συνισαμα
τιχμια· τοοικειοφρα τα μαλαχων· και το υι λαοσυ πευτασε κπος προ απο πον ταπομε νεοσ
απο του προκοπιον συ επαραλαμων· το ταραμ πος καθρορε πι παρα του μαραον κραυ καπε χο
μερου ρ επολιορκησε· και παι ταγουε ναντω λαονε ξηυδραπο αισαλο·

ΛΦΩΝΔΕΠΙΛΑΤΕΟΤΙΕΚΤΗΟΕΞΟΥΟΙΑΟΗΡΩΔΟΥΕΟΤΙΝΑΝΕΠΕΜΨΕΝΑΥΤΟ
ΡΟΟΗΡΩΔΗΝΟΝΤΑΚΑΙΑΥΤΟΝΕΝΙΕΡΟΟΟΛΥΜΟΙΟΕΝΤΑΥΤΑΙΟΤΑΙΟΗΜΕΡΑΙΟ

ΒΑΡΑΒ
ΒΑΟ

ΤΟΙΟΛΡΧΙΕΡΕΥΟΙΝΕΙΟΙΚΑΤΕΡΓΑΗΝΗΓΑΤΕΚΑΙΝΕΙΟΚΑΤΗΓΕΟ

Troy, described by Byron as 'High barrows without marble or a name, a vast untilled, and mountain-skirted plain'; today only earthen mounds, scraps of wall and a jarring replica of the Wooden Horse attempt to summon Hector's glory.

The Rossano Codex: a sixth-century illumination, depicting Pontius Pilate offering the crowds a choice of Christ or Barabbas.

Istanbul: the mosque of Haghia Sophia and the city at night seen
from the harbour. 'Stamboul, peerless of cities, thou jewel beyond
compare,/Seated astride upon two seas, with dazzling light aflare!'
in the words of Ahmet Nedim (1681–1730).

residences and 1800 aristocratic villas. The fifth century also produced sieges and attacks – Alaric in 410 – riots, uncertainty, plague and, in 498, rival popes. The contest between Lawrence and Symacchus brought violence to the streets. As Symacchus, accused of adultery, fled to a refuge outside the city walls, Lawrence's supporters, including senators, went on a murderous rant. They killed anyone suspected of being against their man, they cleared the convents of all nuns and novices, they stripped and publicly whipped women in the streets, and they slaughtered clergy. A legate sent by Theodoric settled the matter: Symacchus became the recognized Pope, Lawrence was given a bishopric.

In the sixth century Rome was captured, liberated, captured again, liberated again. In 536 Belisarius, Justinian's other great general, had freed it in celebratory style – with the agreement of the small Gothic garrison. The Gothic King Vitiges, however, raised an army of 150,000 men and returned to besiege the city for a year and nine days. The siege was lifted by reinforcements sent in by Justinian, and Belisarius set about rebuilding the city and restoring strong defences along the 'twelve miles and three hundred and forty-five paces' of walls. In 546 Totila the Ostrogoth, showing great military skill, besieged the city, using among other devices a fireship floated along the Tiber. Totila was eventually admitted to the city by treacherous sentries, who found the place virtually empty of troops and the people reduced by starvation. When Narses defeated Totila at Tagina, he marched on Rome and freed it once more. During Justinian's reign Rome had experienced five violent changes of fortune – in 536, when Belisarius claimed it for the Empire; in 546, when Totila's Ostrogoths threatened to level it; the following year, when Belisarius recaptured it; in 549, when it was again taken by Totila; and in 552, when Narses rode in after his defeat of Totila. The debilitation had mounted; the city had been riven with famine and mayhem little more than a century before the Skelligs monk walked in. The great St Benedict had taken part in a conversation during the siege of 546, in which a bishop from Constantinople had gloomily forecast that Rome would be so destroyed as to become uninhabited. Benedict contradicted him, saying that, 'Rome will never be depopulated by the barbarians but will be reduced by the natural disasters of storms, earthquakes and lightning, and will decline of her own accord.'

Whatever the ruins the pilgrim monk found – and the city, its aqueducts clogged with weeds and debris, had at one time shrunk to a population of not much more than thirty or forty thousand people from, at its height, a million – one building in Rome, the Pantheon, stood strong, its dignity and firmness still unimpaired to this day. The height of the building has majesty. That quiet massive portico, with its curious air of modesty, those granite columns, have retained more meaning than the embrasures of the Colosseum, as if the gods knew their own worth and on this site at least needed no exaggerating splurge. Up through the centre of the dome the *oculus*, in sunlight, looks like a circle of blue. No glass, no man-made interference – the roof had been kept open so that the sun came straight in and illuminated the statues of the gods in their niches. The disc of golden sunlight on the floor, beamed down from the *oculus*, travels across the paving of the interior as the sun traverses the skies.

Enter a monk of the Dark Ages, come to visit the See of Peter: '*Tu es Petrus.*' In 687 any priest, abbot or bishop travelling the roads of Europe understood that, Arianism notwithstanding, all roads led to Rome. The rock on which the Church had been built may have been quivering, but to the wandering pilgrim, with his beggar's wooden staff and his strong leather shoes, replaced or refurbished along the way, the visible Head of his Church, his Christ's representative on earth, dwelt in the Eternal City. The impression, shaken at times by ambivalent rulers such as Theodoric, or by nervous emperors in Constantinople who feared the influence of the Church in secular matters, had been reinforced massively by the figure of Gregory the Great, who dominated Rome and the Papacy, not only from 590 to 604 but for centuries afterwards.

Gregory was born into a Roman senatorial household, one of those families where authority and the obligation to govern had been almost a matter of genetics: a forefather had been Pope in the previous century. He entered the public service, and at the age of thirty-three he was appointed by the Emperor to the senior civil post in the city's administration, that of *Praetor*, the prefect of Rome. He knew fully the extent of his city's degradation, and wrote,

She that had once been the mistress of the world [has been] shattered by everything that she has suffered from immense and manifold misfortunes – the desolation of her inhabitants and the menace of her enemies. Ruins on ruins, without senate, without people and for that which survives nothing but sorrows and moanings increasing daily. Rome is deserted and burning, and we can only stand by and watch as her buildings collapse of their own accord . . . .

Gregory resigned from his secular duties, became a monk, founded a chain of monasteries inspired by his great contemporary Benedict of Monte Cassino, and entered one which he established in his father's house in Rome. In 579 the resident Pope, Pelagius II, made Gregory his legate to Constantinople, with a specific brief to solicit help from the Emperor in the defence of Rome: the Exarch of Ravenna had refused, saying that he could barely defend his own walls. The Emperor paid no attention to Gregory, but in 590, five years after he returned from Constantinople, Gregory was elected Pope. He immediately broke new intellectual ground within the Church by calling himself 'the servant of the servants of God', and turned the Papacy into an unprecedented institution of charity: Gregory believed, that as an abbot takes responsibility for the spiritual and physical care of his monks, so the Papacy should protect the people.

Bede called Gregory 'a man renowned for learning and behaviour', an opinion with which history unhesitatingly concurs, though it flatters Gregory's own view of himself. He suffered from gout, poor digestion and malaria, which he quelled with quantities of retsina. A slight man, average height, bald with a brown fringe – his biographer studied the family portraits – he had brown eyes and supercilious eyebrows, and a high colour. Self-conscious about his appearance, he believed himself to be feeble, said he was 'an ape obliged to act like a lion' and had superb qualities as an administrator. His impact upon the Church reached far, wide and deep. As well as sending Augustine to Canterbury, he attempted the abolition of slavery, reformed the liturgy, clarified the rubrics and procedures for public ceremonials, reinforced the idea of music as part of worship, stressed the glories of chanted office, and established in the Church an administration that laid the foundations of its later considerable power. His governance of the Church's missions might have been a new Roman Empire: like some spiritual Caesar he looked to the farther world as the generals of old Rome had sought colonies. He administered the Church's treasuries and estates to guarantee funding for the maintenance and blunt evangelical spread of the Roman version of Christianity. (He also believed that the pain of childbirth made women pay for the pleasure of sexual intercourse, and he suggested that all men should 'love women as if their sisters and flee them as if their enemies'.)

During Gregory's reign the Lombards continued their unbridled campaigns. He negotiated with them, especially with Agilulf, the Duke of Spoleto, even while referring to him as 'unspeakable'. Gregory's duty, as he saw it, lay in ensuring that the right climate existed for the spread of the Catholic faith and for the military and political protection of his flock in his capacity as Bishop of Rome. In 592 Agilulf embarked upon a campaign which took him as far as Naples; he captured towns such as Perugia, thus cutting off the direct route between Rome and the exarchate in Ravenna. Gregory succeeded in arranging a treaty with Agilulf, whose wife, Theudelinda, had been a confidante of his, and he then wrote the Queen a letter of thanks for her part in the peace negotiations: 'Nor was it to be expected otherwise from your Christianity but that you would show to all your labour and your goodness in the cause of peace.' To her husband, the unruly Lombard, Gregory wrote: 'Wherefore we strongly praise the prudence and goodness of your Excellency, because in loving peace you show that you love God who is its author. If it had not been made, which God forbid! what could have happened but that the blood of the wretched peasants, whose labour helps us both, would be shed to the sin and ruin of both parties.' This immensely skilled diplomat left hardly a possibility of his office untouched, and he embarked on many initiatives avoided by his predecessors: indeed, his peace treaty with Spoleto angered the Emperor and the Exarch, who understood quite clearly the political and secular precedent that Gregory had set on behalf of the Papacy. All of this happened less than a hundred years before my monk arrived in Rome. The brilliance of Gregory's papal reign still informed the seventh-century Church: in Gregorian chant, in the role that religious played in the life of the Papacy, in the formalized recognition and general tightening of the structures of monasticism.

The Irish monk walked into a Rome where occasionally an ancient, once brilliant building fell into a street without warning. Thieves stole such metal pipes and bronze statues as remained; residents or newcomers building houses carried away chunks of marble and stone from monuments, public buildings and uninhabited villas. Services had broken down substantially, leading to black markets in food and domestic essentials. Water shortages created health hazards – few of the original aqueducts had been restored to anything like their former efficiency. Rows upon rows of houses were empty, though some had been squatted in or simply taken over by the descendants of refugees of earlier wars. Fevers started like lightning, without warning, and ran like wildfire through the city: mortality ran as high as poverty. In 664 the depredations of the Emperor Constans II, a petulant, vicious and hated ruler, had ruinous effects. He took whatever metal he could find, the statues, the railings, the roofs, the props and ties of the great monumental walls, and melted them down to make weaponry. He drowned in his bath, clubbed on the head by a vase in a servant's hand, and the weather carried on with the erosion of the Eternal City.

By the end of the seventh century, a most arresting contrast had grown up between the ragged life of this decaying city and the pomp of any rituals which included the Pope. The Church ceremonies had developed a flavour which spoke of more exotic fashions in worship, a feeling of the Eastern Church. In 687 a new pope took the throne, again amid a dispute. Pope Conon died, and two prelates, the archdeacon Paschal and the archpriest Theodore, offered themselves. Stubbornness prevailed and the deadlock was broken only with the introduction of a third candidate, a Syrian priest living in Naples called Sergius. Despite Paschal's attempt to bribe the Emperor's representative in an effort to prevent the ratification of the election, Sergius's consecration went ahead. He augmented the procedures which had begun with earlier popes anxious to lend the papal court some of the pomp of imperial ceremonial at Constantinople. In Sergius's reign music took on an even greater significance: he had been educated as a cantor. The prelates assisting the new Pope capitalized on his Eastern sense of ceremony. A papal trip to a church other than St Peter's – such as the basilica of Santa Maria Maggiore – became a major event, staged and stage-managed, with different grades of vestments and a series of impressive protocols which further aggrandized the Papacy.

The Pantheon and Santa Maria Maggiore served me as twin outposts – one ancient and pagan, one relatively new and Christian – of a city and an empire which had brought to bear upon the world two immeasurable influences, one secular, one spiritual. I know no other city that can repay the walker so handsomely: I walked from the Pantheon to the great railway station, crossing first of all the Corso. My route took me under the shadows of the Quirinale Palace, with the high flights of steps and, in the alleyways, the old, unexpected fountains that characterize Rome. Old women wearing ancient black sat in their doorways, just looking. The men on the streets had the faces of senators, and the shops, even here, a few paces off one of the most glamorous and lauded streets in the world, sold, like villages, salami and tin openers. Between the Via XX Settembre and the Via Nazionale high, dated bureaucratic offices, closing for the afternoon, stuck handwritten notices, usually cancellations, on the windows. The civil servants of Rome work here, in the Telecommunications Ministry, the Quirinale itself, the Interior Ministry, the Agriculture and Forestry Ministry, the Finance and Defence Ministries, managing the country, while politicians exchange government.

The basilica of Santa Maria Maggiore represented in Rome one of the first examples of the kind of decorative power which Ravenna made famous. Regrettably, the mosaics, higher and farther away than those of Ravenna, cannot be seen as distinctly. The interior has the same high coolness and wide architecture of the contemporary San Vitale in Ravenna. Many claim that this church, rather than San Giovanni in Laterano, should be Rome's cathedral. The basilica has had many internal alterations since the first construction, though the edifice which materializes hugely past the corner of the Via Cavour into the Piazza Esquilino belongs in principle to the fifth century. Santa Maria Maggiore was built by Pope Sixtus III, who blessed Patrick's mission to Ireland in 432, and had to survive arraignment on charges of seducing nuns – his defence quoted Christ (speaking in rather different circumstances): 'Let him who is without sin cast the first stone.'

The night before, as Rome steamed, I had walked from my small *pensione* near the Justice Ministry across the Ponte Sisto to Trastevere to see an even older church. Santa Maria in Trastevere has a more solemn and reclusive air. It is earlier than Maggiore by either one or two centuries, according to differing versions, and it also claims to have initiated church dedication, in

Rome at least, to the Virgin Mary. Mustier and smaller than Maggiore, the original has suffered many superimpositions, amounting to an almost complete rebuilding at various stages down through the centuries. Notwithstanding that, in the church's gloom there shines a Byzantine influence which may not even have been included in the original designs – the gold background and mosaic illuminations come from a much later period.

Pope Sergius I ascended the throne in the year 687 and ruled until 701. His name rarely appears in any high profile among the history of the Papacy, yet the Church owes him a debt for an action which, if he had not taken it, could have changed the entire course of Catholicism. Despite considerable pressure, including the sending of troops, Sergius held out against the demands of the Emperor Justinian II who wanted Constantinople to have equal status in the Church with Rome. The army marching upon Sergius mutinied: the officer in charge of the mission fled for his life and hid – under Sergius's bed.

In Rome by the end of the seventh century successive popes had given themselves a viable Church. By then it had consolidated, turning into a powerful institution, a new European influence, which had created and defended its own credibility. Rocky and scandalous times lay ahead but it had already survived political, military and doctrinal turbulence, even though the means of such survival had often included unthinkable immorality. With each further phase of survival the committed priests and faithful became more assured that the Lord's will protected them. The city even now, especially viewed in the precincts of St Peter's, has the air of a liturgical Washington. Power, even in the service of God, has the same seekers: lofty spiritual ideals do not conceal the wish to influence great numbers of people all over the world. The Church which serves the poor and the needy and the sick and the maimed and the underprivileged has at the centre of operations a sense of power as absolutely sought as in any governed secular society, a legacy directly traceable to Gregory the Great. A Roman Empire still exists, with the same interest in colonization, however different its currency may be.

This child shall enter into the life of the gods, behold them
Walking with antique heroes, and himself be seen of them.
And rule a world made peaceful by his father's virtuous acts.
Child, your first birthday presents will come from nature's wild –
Small presents: earth will shower you with romping ivy, foxgloves,
Bouquets of gypsy lilies, and sweetly-smiling acanthus.
Goats shall walk home, their udders taut with milk, and nobody
Herding them: the ox will have no fear of the lion:
Silk-soft blossom will grow from your very cradle to lap you.

VIRGIL *Eclogues*
trans. Cecil Day-Lewis

CHAPTER FIVE

WALKING
WITH
ANTIQUE
HEROES

O N THE LAST STRETCH of his *peregrinatio* the monk had to find a
Roman road, to take him where he wanted to go. In Rome,
despite its grassy ruins and gap-toothed monuments, the pope
enjoyed an emperor's kind of status; the worship of God smacked of the
East. To a humble pilgrim who had completed his quiet examination of
Peter's Rock, Rome governed the Church and Constantinople governed
Rome. So, *quo vadis*? The question applied intellectually as well as
geographically: difficult for an intelligent man not to enquire further into
his faith, given what he had now seen and heard since Ireland.

The history alone of the development of the Church's teachings had
immense attractions for the questioning mind. The centuries after Peter had
bred controversy after controversy. Those that failed, however well
founded intellectually, or well argued theologically, became heresies; these
habitually arose in places remote from Rome – North African Christians,
for example, stirred several volatile discussions. The Church, centralizing
in Rome, with the imperial assistance of Constantinople, reinforced itself
spiritually, intellectually and sometimes physically: Pope Sixtus III built
Santa Maria Maggiore as a response to the decisions of the Council of

Ephesus in 431, one of the many convocations at which the early Church laid down the principles by which it still governs itself.

The scriptures, containing the biography of Jesus Christ and the history of his times, had become holy writ, accepted, transcribed into illuminated manuscripts, memorized, analysed and discussed. The life of Christ, and his miracles and his teachings, had become a broad strand in the Church's literature. The dominant discussion during the third and fourth centuries after Christ's death dwelt on his nature as Man and God, the human and the divine, and, if both, in what sequence or proportion. Donatists and Montanists and Docetists and Monarchianists and Sabelianists argued – and were often massacred for it – along multifarious lines, a typical example being the thought that, as God, Jesus Christ did not suffer the agony of the Passion, since he had a divine being, or, if he did not suffer, he did not have a divine being, he therefore was not God. These divisions, denounced by the Church as heretical, multiplied; many were promulgated by those who lived outside society – extreme sects, fugitives, refugees. In the late fourth century Filastrius, Bishop of Brescia, stated that as a result of his researches he could identify 156 such dissenting voices existing within Christianity.

The question asked by Arius of Alexandria – whether Christ, having had a beginning in birth, therefore did not have the necessary attribute of God 'in whom there is no beginning and no end' – stimulated the Council of Nicea in 325. Constantine the Great, as well as convening Nicea, further helped the Roman Catholic view by stamping out any examples he found of polytheism, its oracles and auguries. In 394 on the calendar employed by Bede, Pelagius, a Briton, thought to be a Welshman otherwise called Morgan, 'spread far and near the infection of his perfidious doctrine against the assistance of Divine Grace ... St Augustine, and the other orthodox fathers, quoted many authorities against them, yet they would not correct their madness.' Pelagius, though his views on human perfectibility seem developmental and humanistic, got short and abusive shrift from the old men of the Church. Bede wrote:

> A scribbler vile, inflamed with hellish spite
> Against the great Augustine dared to write
> Presumptuous serpent! from what midnight den
> Darest thou crawl on earth and look at men?

Ephesus, in 410, the third ecumenical council (from *oecumenicus*, or *oikoumenikos*, meaning the whole, inhabited earth) became the battlefield in another long schismatizing war. It broke down into two essential schools of thought – those, supported by Rome, who believed that within Christ had existed the perfect union of God and Man, the human and the divine, against those led by Nestorius, Bishop of Constantinople, who, by contrast, emphasized the human manhood of Christ. This view would have denied Mary (who, legendarily, had been buried at Ephesus) the accolade of having borne God. The Roman Church, which crudely routed the Nestorian view, then affirmed its devotion to the cult of Mary the mother of God – hence the building of Santa Maria Maggiore. Rome banished Nestorius, but his thesis evolved into a separate and widely divisive strand of belief, which long prospered in Syria, Persia and Iraq, and whose adherents even took Christianity to India and China.

Certain circumstances of the Council of Ephesus were repugnant. The opponents of Nestorius dismayed those who believed that churchmen should set exemplary standards. They bribed the local clergy and hierarchy, reviled and threatened those who advocated the beliefs of the much-respected Nestorius, lobbied the gathering prelates shamelessly, and brought forward the convening of the Council in an attempt to force the issue before Nestorius's allies arrived from the East. The caring spirit, as exemplified later by Gregory, put in no appearance in these early matters of the primitive Church. When Nestorius eventually died a rival said, 'The living on earth rejoice; the dead regret his death, fearing that they may have to endure association with him. Let those who bury him lay him beneath a large gravestone, lest his deceitful spirit rise again. May he take his teachings to Hell, where he will doubtless entertain the damned from morning to night.'

The faith adhered to by the monks of western Europe followed, therefore, the simple rules laid down by Rome – that Jesus Christ, born of Mary, was the Son of God sent to earth to redeem humanity, and that he was sacrificed by God in this cause, that he ascended to Heaven and that Peter, his fisherman, created the Church to carry on the work of salvation. The Gospels of the Four Evangelists made this understanding available to humanity, and the Rome of the popes carried it forward as uncomplicatedly as possible. Nevertheless, the monk from the Skelligs wanted to find out more, wanted to see the East, hear other voices, see the colours of other vestments – already in Rome much more vivid even than those in France – wanted to view further the spirit he had found in Ravenna and naturally expected to find an enlargement of it at Constantinople. On the way he could survey what fragments he found of the Greek classical world.

Ivory panel, possibly carved by craftsmen in Rome, showing the
Hippodrome in Constantinople.

The journey, first to Brindisi, then onwards eastwards, filled up with mixed fortunes. The territory below Rome, scarcely recorded during the Dark Ages when it lay under the control of the Lombard dukes of Spoleto and Beneventum, contained some, but not much, relevant history – whereas yet again those periods which proved irrelevant had immense fascination. The first – obvious – destination, Monte Cassino, provided an immediate overshadow of later events. The early view of the monastery, seen from many miles away, way up on the heights, brings back the memories of all those post-war grainy black-and-white photographs of the Allied bombardment in 1944, when it was believed to be a German redoubt. As pounded as Dresden, the building now offers no visual rewards at all. Neither does the interior, and the place has no hint of ancient thrill befitting the fountainhead of such a powerful cultural development. I shall most remember the arid din of the cicadas, deafening on the hard climb, reaching unpleasant crescendoes on each turn of the road. Skellig Michael contained far more natural piety in its wild stones than the corridors and innumerable windows of Monte Cassino.

The war must have done this. Before the bombardments an atmosphere of ancient devotion must, surely, have been available here? The disappointing shallowness resonated so forcibly that when I did see a monk crossing the concourse I momentarily took him for a visitor too. The war memorial on the hill contained more spiritual intensity than the entire monastery, and the view across the valley, clear and without haze on a brilliant morning, also offered more to the spirit – the white cemeteries said more than the chants of the monks inside, even though they still follow in the footsteps of the man who endowed the world with his sensible and impressive *Regula Monachorum* in this place in 515.

On the way up to the monastery, the town beneath had a more hostile and closed atmosphere than any Italian town I have ever visited. Perhaps the citizens have long memories, in which case they have good reason for gathering their folds surlily about them – who knows what ruin from the air strangers may bring? A breakfast of coffee and chocolate turned out to be a matter of silence and brooding. Within a few hundred yards of the town's pine-straggled edge, the silence grew official in the rows of white crosses of the many cemeteries. Those ordered acres yielded multitudes of Irish names, Ruane, MacCarthy, O'Brien; if any truth lies in my recurring impression that places of turbulence retain their violence, this place, by virtue of the antiseptic decency in which they have dressed it, had an unencompassable awfulness.

Benedict, who founded Christianity's most influential monastery, came from Norcia, one of those mosquito-happy hill villages near Spoleto in Umbria, and as a teenage boy chose mortification by living in a cave near Subiaco beyond Rome. The reputation of such piety gave him the customary stature among clerics; he advanced in the ranks of the Church and at the behest of the local hierarchy became an abbot. 'And when he had come here,' wrote Paul the Deacon, 'that is to the citadel of Cassinum, he always restrained himself in great abstinence, but especially at the time of Lent he remained shut up and removed from the noise of the world.' Benedict had ambition, and he fulfilled it by expressing disapproval for the unruliness of contemporary monastic orders. European monks still followed Coptic and even earlier traditions, and, despite substantial leaps forward in the definition of dogma, much of the structure of monastic life, both practical and spiritual, lacked clarification. Benedict adopted a position which, viewed now, has the hallmarks of that early, developing Christianity, and can even be seen to mirror the new statement on the nature of Christ – that is to say, he insisted upon a wedding of the spiritual and the physical, as if to echo the human and divine in Christ. If the object of the monastic life were to be devotion, Benedict believed, then practical arrangements must permit that devotion to be observed.

One of his major themes ordained that 'Idleness is the enemy of the soul.' With this one moral stroke he transformed the lives of men who followed God, lifted the monastic life out of the rough and elevated it to a kind of spiritual art form, in which every gesture had a creative motive – creative, that is, in the love and service of God. To establish this new and revolutionary monasticism – a break with, and vast improvement upon, the more haphazard rule of the past – he took followers from his abbacy and began with the discipline of time. Every house of what would become the Benedictine Order had to observe a timetable, a full roster of prayer and practical duty. He applied the good sense of an executive to ensure that if the monks could be kept occupied when not at prayer, the quality of their communal life – often, hitherto, not far above the habits of the wild – would improve. At the same time, he ordained that silence – what he termed *taciturnitas*, a general disposition towards the condition of eschewing talk – should be observed as widely as practicably possible: a shrewd thought, it promoted contemplativeness and proved helpful in the preservation of harmony in such enclosed communities.

The basic ingredients of Benedict's Rule could be applied to any group of people desirous of a disciplined, thoughtful life, in any surroundings, in any culture. Benedict took a few fundamental requirements necessary to the maintenance of human survival and supportive of personal dignity, and with them he gave monks permission to live safely, without unnecessary eccentricity, savage denial or any other pietistic extravagance. In other words, he took simple human conditions for community life and elevated them to a Rule. For instance, he encouraged monks towards sensible and regularized clothing, with changes of shift, tunic, cowl, stockings and shoes. Each man had the right to take care of himself without running the risk of being called materialistic, or self-aggrandizing; a man could keep his clothes neat and clean and tidy and not be charged with lacking the gift of self-mortification. No private property could be held: the clothing and the bedding, though used individually, belonged in common, along with the utensils of the monastery, the pen in the *scriptorium*, the hoe in the field.

Food had to be of a good and standard quality, not elaborate, yet nutritious, the victuals of the local countryside and people. The cooking of the food took on a new importance: the monks grew and boiled their own vegetables, and with fruit and their own bread they supplemented this largely vegetarian diet, which sometimes included fish and poultry, but rarely red meat. The monks devised diets and medicines for those who ailed, and it became a privilege of almost holy dimensions to serve a sick brother or sister. The stringent self-mortifications of the anchorites fell quietly out of favour, as it transpired that health and energy contributed to a more vigorous worship of God. Severe discipline prevailed, with corporal punishments for such serious offences as attempting to have any form of personal possession – members of the community had to submit to searches.

The central control of this life revolved around the rota. A time to rise, a time to pray and a time to meditate, a time to work and a time to eat, a time to study and a time to fast, a time to recreate and a time to retire – the Rule of Benedict became, effectively, an innovative strand of civilization which he designed in a way that permitted the human capacity for worship to be maximized. It adapted widely and connected with the growing common sense of civilized man, which understood that to pursue the spirit successfully the body had to be put in order. The Rule stood up under investigation, with its sensible mix of prayer and work. It could be criticized neither for severity nor for laxity. It applied – to the great relief of those who embraced it anew, coming from other directions, with previous experience – boundaries to human conduct which did not test them to unbearable levels, and yet permitted them to be devout. For the sake of accessibility it had been written in vernacular Latin.

The Church, once it understood the principles, embraced Benedict and his Rule, gave this new monasticism its enthusiastic blessing and protected Benedictines when they came under fire. Gregory led the enthusiasm. When the Lombards attacked Monte Cassino in the late sixth century, one of the documents which the fleeing monks remembered to save was Benedict's Rule. When it came into the hands of Gregory it answered his need for a standardized monastic policy within the Church. Benedict had died in 547, excellent timing for a biographical work consistent with the widespread principle of hagiography, and Gregory undertook this: the book became famous and popular for many centuries. He also advanced energetically the cause of Benedictinism, urging it upon the various – particularly the Western – provinces of the Church. Any late seventh-century Irish monk on his *peregrinatio*, if not already converted to Benedictinism, would have been giving Benedict's Rule the most serious consideration. It had begun to spread in the sees that such a monk passed through, in the monasteries where he had stayed, through France and Germany, and he could compare it with two other great rules he had encountered, those of Columba in Iona and of Columbanus, still remembered at St Gallen. A survey of the Benedictine way of life, and in Cassino itself – though the monastery had suffered enough hostility from marauding princes to disrupt its occupation – would provoke in a *peregrinus* a re-examination of the monkish life.

The south, where as in Umbria I longed to linger again, has a different quality. Robert Browning called it 'the land of lands' and dreamed of houses where

> ... for ever crumbles
> Some fragment of the frescoed walls,
> From blisters where a scorpion sprawls.
> A girl bare-footed brings, and tumbles
> Down on the pavement, green-flesh melons ...

In the monk's time Virgil's poems still had currency and distinction, especially in the courts of Naples, where he had lived, and in the minds of religious scholars pondering the eclogue he wrote forecasting the birth of a child who would inaugurate a new Golden Age.

> This boy will be accepted into the life of the gods, will view them
> Walking with antique heroes, and himself be seen as one of them
> And will rule a world pacified by the virtues of his father.

The Messianic Eclogue provoked wide discussion among Church scholars. Did Virgil appear to prophesy the birth of Christ? Even in the Middle Ages mystical qualities were still being attributed to Virgil, and those lines contained much comfortable room for Christian interpretation, no matter how otherwise pagan Virgil's era seemed.

The names of these regions of the south, however obscure their Dark Ages history may be, echo ancient events. Ancient Capua (now called Santa Maria in Capua Vetere) has a Roman amphitheatre which preserves the mood of the circus. Satellite X-ray photographs might reveal early patterns of land division just beneath the surface of the earth. Three hundred years before Christ Rome began a system of colonization here, by allotting plots of land to over two thousand families. Capua had the status of second city and, though established by the Etruscans, became coveted by Rome for its strategic position, twelve miles from the sea, and for its fertility. In later centuries a beleaguered and besieged Rome often commandeered the harvests of Capua and Campania.

Outside the town, my frustration set in once more: regrettably, the Italians do not always flag the sites of their early battles. I could not trace the spot where, in 554, Narses the eunuch won a famous victory along these riverbanks over Bucellinus, one of two barbarian brothers who raided Italy with an army of 75,000 German warriors. On the banks of the Volturno Narses laid a trap into which marched the barbarians in a wedge of fighting men, mainly infantry, carrying throwing-axes and javelins, for hand-to-hand combat. In a circle on their flanks rode the Roman archers, fully armoured, out of reach, deadly and, in the brilliantly engineered circumstances, invincible.

Naples in the Dark Ages received a battering as severe as Rome, if not more catastrophic. It commanded a position of crucial usefulness, a port where reinforcements from other parts of the Empire could land. It suffered heavily during Justinian's attempts to remove the Gothic influence from the government of Italy. In 536 Belisarius, after a campaign in Africa, returned to southern Italy across the Straits of Messina. Those towns in Gothic hands surrendered until he came to Naples, where the citizens explained their dilemma: their mixed Gothic and Roman population had grown so integrated that any attack by Belisarius upon the city would throw it into confusions of loyalty. They argued that he should ignore the city, which, if he took Rome, would automatically become part of the Empire. But Belisarius reasoned that the strategic importance of Naples as a garrison and a port warranted the confirmation of the city as part of Justinian's restored Empire. He laid siege, eventually got through along a water channel, breached the gates and sacked the city. In 542 Totila in his turn levelled its walls. Naples remained a prize, a fact which ensured continuous aggression, which sometimes led to the city being divided equally between Gothic and imperial interests, as well as being cut off from both Rome and Ravenna. From here, his detractors alleged, Narses sent for the Lombards when he fell out of favour with the new Byzantine Empress. From here in 664 Constans, frustrated at his impotence against the Lombards of Beneventum, set out for Rome on his mission to strip the city of its remaining valuables. What is true of Naples is true of Italy as a whole in these centuries. Byzantium's attempts to bring it back within the imperial fold, and the bloody campaigns that accompanied them, in the end fragmented and then eroded Roman culture in the peninsula.

Records kept in Naples attempt to trace every known murmur of Vesuvius. The eruption in 685 amounted to no more than a cough, a short paroxysm, with little of the force of previous eruptions, such as the one in 472 whose ash had been borne on the west wind as far to the east as Constantinople itself – and certainly none of the lava flow that four centuries earlier eclipsed Pompeii and Herculaneum. By 687 Pompeii, along with Herculaneum, constituted not much more than a race memory, with both towns stratified under solidified volcanic rock which would not be excavated with any organized concentration for another eleven hundred years. The lore of Vesuvius, however, could easily have formed part of the conversation of the monasteries. The farmers – monks among them – knew when the mountain stirred: the animals whinged and shifted, the birds flew away from the area, gaseous and unpleasant smells filled the air, the sun darkened and the earth trembled: dreadfully comforting portents for a man of faith who had read of the momentous events which marked Calvary. The pagan stories also thrilled: for days before the great eruptions the people could see huge men walking about high up on the rim of the crater, or flying through the air and alighting on the mountain's saucer peak, and then wandering and clambering gigantically through the rocks and the scrub. These gigantic, unreal figures later populated the black smoke that poured up out of the mountain; to the sound of terrible trumpets they swirled about within the smoke, gods and dervishes at once, as the awful rivers of rock and mud raced down the slopes.

I knew full well that the monk could not have seen any of Pompeii – all he saw was black landscape, overgrown where the grass found it possible, where a stunted shrub got a foothold – yet I could not resist digressing there. At seven o'clock in the morning the workmen, with the aid of some lire, proved obliging. In a deserted little street, which has yet to receive the full attentions of twentieth-century archaeology and restoration, the deep chariot ruts in the paving stones whistled up at once the *frisson* of Pompeii.

Away from these small artisan areas, the great villas had decorations of a standard according to the family's wealth and cultural awareness. Extensive use of colour, with an Egyptian red prominent, and the employment of *trompe l'oeil* and animal and erotic images gave Pompeii an early sophistication and distinction. The statuary, the painting and the general quality of work such as the famous ithyphallic tripod – three satyrs in an exaggeratedly happy state holding up a bronze bowl, now in the Museo Nationale on the Piazza Cavour in Naples – portray Pompeii as a rich and relaxed town, full of money and education, with a confident economy and a stable, middle-class society from which many inhibitions had been expelled. By 687, throughout Italy, such societies had been swept away as thoroughly as if they too had been in the shadow of Vesuvius.

Along the platform in the great arched railway station at Naples, hawkers sold food in small baskets – half bottles of wine, fat rounds of bread, some fruit, some ham, cheese. They handed the baskets up to carriage doors several steps above them. The bread proved too hard to eat, the wine too warm and thin to drink, the *prosciutto* too leathery, the fruit too old. The crowded train had severe old women in the inevitable black, grinning soldiers, some nuns and children. These Italian trains, more pronouncedly in the south, leave the station with a degree of ceremony and like departing guests have the good manners not to put on any momentum until they have attained a respectable distance from the terminus. The train jerked past signposts to Eboli where Christ stopped unpityingly, thus rendering the region poorer than the poor, and at Potenza I changed to a small, two-carriage train.

The train journey, long, diverse and awkwardly slow, offered little opportunity for anything but reflection. The road of this Dark Ages pilgrim had for the first time veered towards the improbable: in Britain and France and Switzerland and Italy as far as Rome, records existed to confirm such pathways – the pilgrims who trod this land south of Rome had been travelling in the opposite direction: to, not from, the Eternal City. This raised questions about the nature of the *peregrinus*, or rather about the social tempo which observed him, encouraged him and celebrated him.

To begin with, he came from a tradition which ensured that he stood apart, in some cases spectacularly so; holy men included those who had visibly conquered the demands of the body by achieving triumphant feats of self-denial, such as Simeon Stylites or Jerome or the motley desert fathers. Their performance of their chosen lives had entered the race memory of both Christianity at large and that of the monastic life. The Irish monk of the period was describing a curious full circle which connected him to the asceticism by which the holy man of Byzantine times had gained his reputation. The famed demonstrativeness of the hermits in the Syrian desert was replicated, though in less heat and with fewer spectators, by those who lived on Skellig Michael or in the beehive huts of Kerry, or like St Cuthbert who took to an isle off Lindisfarne. From the available accounts, the western hermits did not seem to behave as flamboyantly as, say, Simeon on his stylus, or the anchorite with his pet lion whom Jewish travellers met and reported to Theodoret, the historian Bishop of Cyrrhus. On the extreme edges of the Byzantine Empire, however, traditions existed of severe religious expression on the parts of individual monks who had then banded themselves into groups, either in monasteries such as Skellig Michael, or roaming bands who frequently, out of hunger or wilfulness, smeared themselves across Syrian landscapes. The Benedictine Rule did not begin to take marked effect in western Europe until the ninth century, before which the Irish followed an independent tradition which had sprung from an Egyptian prototype. In the seventh century, a form called *regula mixta* frequently obtained, which combined the practical elements of the Benedictines' monastic persuasion with the purity of the Irish.

By the seventh century, the irregularities which had characterized the earliest holy men had in any case calmed down. The holy man had long come to be regarded for his special powers, such as efficaciousness in illness, both before and after his death, a figure who could bring order out of chaos: Aidan of Lindisfarne controlled vicious human beings as well as unspeakable demons. The holy man could, as Columbanus did when taking on the arduous career of evangelist, draw great numbers of followers, both kings and slaves: this was a new power, comparatively speaking, and a mystical one, beholden to no temporal principles. On the contrary, it gave the holy man the right to interfere, sometimes dramatically, in affairs of state at the highest level – remember how fearlessly Columbanus chided the whoring Theuderic. In all circumstances the monk, religious, monastic or hermit, eventually had a special place, one which he frequently turned to political advantage as in the reign of the Merovingian kings, or as in Gregory's Papacy, when priests became the pope's provincial governors and the lines between religious and secular grew blurred.

On and beyond the western extremities of the Roman Empire, from the beginning, perhaps due to the fixed and accepted position of the Druid in pre-Christian society, an expectation existed, and therefore the emergent figure of the Christian holy man seemed not too egregious. The efficiency with which the early evangelists, such as Palladius and Patrick, organized their missions must have contributed. In small, relatively compact societies a man who chose ascetically and demonstratively to follow the word of

Part of a sixth-century ivory diptych depicting the circus, with an audience in the top corners.

God, which the local king had just accepted, received respect – unlike the less fortunate Eastern figures who were often blamed for making local girls pregnant, or causing crops to fail, or disturbing the weather. In the East, the hermit or anchorite frequently seemed to act as a fantasy *alter ego* which expressed or drew off the shadowy in people's natures; in western Europe he acted as a lightning conductor of the gods-become-God, an agent of efficacy, a conduit of supplication and salvation.

The Irish, and other monks of the Celtic Church, brought a further special dimension to the status of the holy man turned pilgrim. By choice he was often an exile – not a traveller, not a tourist, not a banished person;

his exile had within it a glory and a distinguished tradition, a white, as distinct from a bloody red martyrdom. Such exile – and they used the word calculatedly – originated deliberately. Nobody instructed them or conscripted them; they did not represent their monasteries, nor were they necessarily expected to return. If they gave reasons for their departure it was explained simply as the feeling of having received a divine instruction. 'O, Father,' prayed Boethius, Theodoric's ill-fated philosopher, 'give the spirit power to climb to the fountain of all light and be purified.... Thou carriest us, and Thou doest go before, Thou art the journey and the journey's end.'

At source, the Irish form of *peregrinatio* had a number of forms. These embraced the holy man who wished to make such a journey, like Gallus, for Christ, but whose flesh, through age or infirmity, did not permit. Another category of pilgrim never left the shores of Ireland, but travelled internally, visiting Irish shrines and monasteries. Others travelled to Scotland, to Ninian in Galloway, to Columba on Iona, or to Britain, to the Lindisfarne of Aidan and Cuthbert, perhaps to David in Wales. The elite, if one may use the term, travelled to Europe. Sometimes they carried on missionary work, sometimes not; perhaps, like Egbert, they exiled themselves, temporarily or permanently, as a form of penance, supplication or worship. In 664 Egbert, ailing to the point where he feared death, as the Venerable Bede describes,

went out of his chamber where the sick lay, and sitting alone in a convenient place, began seriously to reflect upon his past actions, and being full of compunction at the remembrance of his sins, bedewed his face with tears, and prayed fervently to God tht he might not die yet, before he could make amends for the offences which he had committed in his infancy and younger years, or might further exercise himself in good works. He also made a vow that he would, for the sake of God, live in a strange place, so as never to return to the island of Britain where he was born....

Not all travellers came from the religious life. Sometimes a *peregrinatio* resulted from a punishment and it applied to several offences – as in the case of the man who visited Columba on Iona, a man who had been accused of committing incest with his mother and murdering a relative. Columba sentenced him to wander until God forgave his sins, because such a man should not, under law, have been allowed to pollute the shores of Iona. An Irish monk wandering the roads of Europe in the seventh century could also have been pursuing enforced exile, banished for a period of penance for intercepting and helping himself, in part or in total, to the gifts intended for his bishop or abbot.

If, for whatever aspect of godliness, the Irish monk of 687 had chosen to travel through these lands to atone for past sins, he must have felt his penance lift the guilt from him. Life runs hard in the south, whatever the sun and the clear sky. Many of the farms remain small, many of the regions are classified close to Third World status by the EEC. Looking out of the window of the hard, two-carriage train, I tried to visualize what the monk saw as he came across these hills, perhaps on horseback, and for his sake I hoped that he had the company of a large wagon train of merchants and their protectors. He travelled through dangerous anarchic lands, though wealthier then than the north – the reverse situation, which today maintains an economic gulf between the poor south and the now much wealthier north of Italy, did not come about until the Norman invasions several centuries later. The countryside, initially comfortable, seemed to me to grow more inhospitable by the mile, even though much farming territory has been won back from the scrubland and, in parts, from the volcanic seashore. By 687 the south of Italy had experienced large and regular influxes of Greek refugees from Islam and the Slavs, including prelates making significant contributions to the affairs of the Church, for instance Pope Sergius I and Theodore of Tarsus, who became Archbishop of Canterbury. My destination, Brindisi, the great port of Brundisium, which today feels as if it could be a Greek as well as an Italian town, has a past which, when scanned chronologically, sums up the history through which the monk walked – with many fleets embarking on brave departures, many hostile landings, many invasions, many returning heroes, many conflicts, even a significant treaty signed in the city.

Two and a half centuries before the birth of Christ, Rome built a colony which capitalized upon Brundisium's geography as a fine natural harbour.

Twin arms of land curved out in a wide embrace, creating a port large enough to contain an effective fleet, with which the Roman generals intended to prevent Carthaginian ships using the Adriatic. It also acted as a launching pad for assaults across the Adriatic, into the land of Illyria, corresponding with modern Yugoslavia and Albania, and into Greece. Forty years before, in 280 BC, King Pyrrhus had ventured out from the north-west of Greece and taken Sicily and the south of Italy. The Illyrians also had to be contained, and when they reacted against the Roman establishment in Brundisium by killing merchants and legates, the Romans attacked the Illyrian queen with considerable success.

On the night of 10 January 49 BC, Julius Caesar changed Roman history by crossing the Rubicon – a physically insignificant, symbolically unforgettable river in north-eastern Italy – and executed an act of civil war. He had only a small army, which he split, and led one half down along the coast to Rimini. His declared opponent, Pompey, had also been his son-in-law (Caesar's daughter, Julia, Pompey's wife, had died five years earlier). Caesar, vastly experienced, pursued the less effective, lazier Pompey down to these parts until Pompey slipped the blockade intended for him in Brundisium.

Virgil, having taken a fever in Athens, died in Brundisium on 21 September 19 BC. He had lived through a most vivid period of Roman history, largely of civil war, and, as a favourite at the courts of the aristocrats, had heard the gossip, the intrigues and the manoeuvres of Caesar and Pompey, Brutus and Cassius, Mark Antony and Cleopatra. Pompey was assassinated when he landed, on the run, in Egypt in 48 BC; Caesar suffered the same fate on the Ides of March 44 BC; and Antony and Cleopatra lost to Octavian in 31 BC.

In the later history of Italy, Brundisium shared many of the destinies of the fluctuating empires, Roman and Byzantine, the raids of the foreign tribes, the establishments of small rulerships, and through the descending centuries it retained the constant state of importance due to such a vital harbour. Long after the monk reached it the Crusaders made it a naval base. In the seventh century it flourished as a valve of trade between Italy and the East, a point of contact, often tumultuous, between the Lombard dukedoms of the south and Byzantium. For four hundred years before the monk arrived in Brundisium Byzantium's brilliant civilization had kept this port busy with trade. For four hundred years before that Rome itself had dominated this sea, and for a further four hundred years before that the Hellenistic civilization, cultural and political, metaphysical and military, exercised its powerful influence throughout much of the Adriatic and eastern Mediterranean.

Brundisium marked a point of marvellous departure for a conservative traveller out of western Europe. Behind him lay a turbulent continent, with a history which he had by now encountered, admittedly in snatches and lore, in glimpses of the life at the courts and in the monasteries and in the streets and farms. Before him, on the last leg of the journey, lay a synthesis, a fusion, of past and future. He had the opportunity to sample the pagan glory of ancient Greece, whose flavour he had tasted in the writings and language of his education – albeit confusedly and well salted with Christianity – and in his conversations with other travellers. The ancient, thrilling past could be surveyed at Delphi, shrine, home and breeding ground of antique heroes, a magnet for travellers and pilgrims since the sixth century before Christ, reached by a long sea crossing from Italy to Greece, from Brindisi to Patras.

Brindisi still has a powerful port and has lost none of its deepwater capacity for large shipping. I arrived late on a Thursday afternoon, when the wind from the sea – how surprisingly threatening the Adriatic looks – kept the town cool. Scaffolding surrounded one of the twin columns which marked the end of the Via Appia, and across the water of the harbour the huge monument to Mussolini, an enormously tall, half-curved, half-flat slab of concrete, looked like the inverted comb of some mad fighting giant bird. Nobody sat in the Piazza del Popolo. Everybody, locals and tourists, had congregated in the street which leads down to the harbour and is lined with agencies selling ferry tickets. Corfu, Patras, Piraeus – the names read like the travelogue of a Homeric adventure, and I embarked with three hundred other foot travellers, mostly backpacking American students.

We left at a few minutes before midnight, two hours late and nobody caring. For an hour I could see the lights behind us, especially the bright glow on top of the Mussolini column. No wonder this harbour had such value to the Roman and then the Byzantine Empire: no fleet could get in here without being seen hours in advance. Ships passed us; the tug, padded with tyres, which chugged by lest we needed guidance and assistance, turned like a unicyclist and belted back to the dockside. Huge ferries, vast bulks, lay at anchor, motionless and lit up inside, light pouring out through their vast embarkation doors and tiny men, toys, standing by.

On deck the American students teemed everywhere – without them the passenger list would have amounted to no more than twenty, a sad-eyed old man, a crisply spoken English businessman who drank hugely for several hours, an Italian honeymoon couple, two couples in cars with Scandinavian registrations, three Italian families travelling together, one Greek priest and a young man from Dublin who had left the seminary because he had decided that he could not take the religious life (his mother had accepted his decision much better than he had ever expected). The Americans partied on the top deck, laughed like urban hyenas and danced to the flashing disco lights. I had to go as far for'ard as the ship's regulations would permit to catch any glimpse of the stars. The night bore on hot and noisy: by morning, when I could not sleep in the hard metal cabin, the Americans had subsided into largely drunken slumbers. In the dawn haze an island appeared in the ferry's sights – Corfu, where many disembarked and walked away into the small town. The ship left the port and headed out again, deeper into the spotlessly clean Ionian Sea. The sun came out, turned as pitiless as the Ancient Mariner's.

At four o'clock in a roasting afternoon we landed at Patras, where Byron first encountered Greece. After Christ's death St Andrew, the second of the apostles, Peter's brother, preached along this coast and in AD 61 was crucified diagonally. His successor as Bishop of Patras, St Regulus, also known as Rule, was told by an angel in a dream that he must end the constant squabbling over the relics of Andrew, take them away and find them a new home. He became a pilgrim traveller, sailed through the Mediterranean and got shipwrecked off the coast of Scotland as part, apparently, of the angel's plan. He founded St Andrews in Scotland – hence the white diagonal cross of Andrew's crucifixion as Scotland's (much later) national flag. So the Scots said, though they are suspected of having tried to compete with the elitism of an English cult of St Peter himself, in whose initiation Bede played a large part. Nor did Rule's journey settle the differences over Andrew's relics. A busy mythology sprang up around the saint, which had his head in one place, his limbs and cross in others, and gave him the credit for founding Contantinople. It also resulted in a rather ugly neo-Byzantine church in Patras called Agios Andreas, where a gold casket is said to hold Andrew's head.

I waited for a local bus to Rio, and a ferry took me on the shorter route to Delphi. A handful of people, with children, stood on the brown wooden deck. The few cars included a van taking across what seemed like the entire fitments of somebody's new bathroom. When the van's wheels stuck in the metal cleats of the ferry after the short crossing everybody, myself included, pushed until it snorted up the ramp where a boy waited, with an old-fashioned barrow on which was mounted a large perspex box from which he sold rings of hard bread studded with sesame seeds.

The road to Delphi wound by the sea, seen through outbreaks of olive and azalea, with islands and lagoons shimmering in the wooded distance. Very early the following morning, from the hills above Delphi, on the side of Parnassus's long harsh escarpment, I walked down through scrubland and olive groves and chickens and early old men with hats and moustaches, down the edge of the mountain to the shrine of Apollo, the navel of the world.

It must be possible that the monk saw this scene more or less as I now did. Delphi had been dismissed, desecrated and closed down, had even suffered enormous depredation, by the late seventh century, but none the less the ruins bulked too large to have disappeared by the time he got there. In later centuries the land covered the shrine almost completely, people built houses on the earth above it, and the site remained largely forgotten and concealed until serious excavations began in the late nineteenth century. In any case, as well as the physical details, which took time and energy to absorb, the religious and historical implications of Delphi could not have been lost on an educated traveller of the seventh century. Whatever his – or anyone else's – spiritual leanings, Delphi's force could never, and still cannot, be ignored.

Delphi existed as a shrine in the time of the Myceneans, from the fourteenth to the tenth century BC. In common with civilizations as geographically far apart as the Mesopotamians and proto-Celts, Delphi then worshipped the goddess of the earth and made offerings to her, in the form of statues made in her – and the supplicant's – likeness. In due course she gave way to Apollo, the sun-god. This beautiful young man, with the classical slim-hipped, broad-chested physique, was born on the island of Delos. He had the conception and birth of a god: sired by Zeus, sharing a womb with Artemis, the goddess of fertility, he sprang forth into the light from the loins of Leto, Zeus's mistress. She had fled to escape the anger of Hera, Zeus's wife – who cursed the pregnant Leto, swearing that she could only bear the children in a place where the sun's rays could not penetrate. Poseidon, god of the seas, raised a canopy of waves over the island, all the Immortals attended and the goddesses gave Apollo a girdle of gold, while feeding him with ambrosia and nectar.

When the child was four days old, he strode off down the slopes of Olympus to establish his shrine. At Parnassus he was attacked by a malevolent female in the form of a serpent, but Apollo killed the dragon and cried aloud, as he watched it writhe to death, 'Rot where you lie.' The serpent rotted, and from the Greek word meaning 'to rot' the name Pytho was given to this rocky grove at the foot of a cascade under the brooding lip of Parnassus. Now that he had a shrine, Apollo needed priests to form his cult. On the sea he saw a ship bound for Corinth from Crete. He assumed the shape of a dolphin, pursued the ship and obliged the crew to forsake their old lives and become the priests and guardians of his temple, and since they first encountered him in the shape of a dolphin they gave the place the name of Delphi.

Apollo became multi-efficacious, capable of calming the seas or vanquishing giants, of making the beasts of the forests dance to his music or single-handedly banishing hostile armies to Hades, of laying the foundations of great new cities and removing the clouds from the sun. His attributes grew – Apollo the omnipotent as well as the beautiful, the peaceful as well as the warrior, replete with grace, strength and eternal youth, with whom the goddesses fell in love. His life, his efficacies, his adventures and his loves embraced almost all the mythological archetypes – he bore one lover away in a golden chariot, children borne by another received protection from the wolves when abandoned in the forest; he sired the father of medicine, Asclepius, gave Cassandra the gift of prophecy and fell in love with Hyacinthus whose blood, from a fatal forehead wound caused by a discus Apollo had thrown in sport but which got misdirected by jealous gods, spurted to the ground and from it sprang the hyacinth flower.

Whenever it was that Apollo selected Delphi as the place for his shrine, his sanctuary was completed in the sixth century BC, and thereafter, for several centuries – until AD 392 when the Emperor Theodosius the Great closed it down – drew enormous numbers of pilgrims. Apollo had chosen the site, nearly two thousand feet above sea level, because Parnassus was exceeded in height only by Mount Olympus itself, and because the place already had a reputation for the purest of air, which came forth directly from a cleft in the earth. Those who breathed in these airs gained the gift of superhuman clairvoyance. Apollo moderated – in the spiritual and political sense – Greek existence and morality by creating greater peace, first of all within the individual, then between neighbouring cities. As an expression of these achievements, and as a means of relaxation and reflection after them, he demonstrated the gentle munificence of the arts by playing the lyre and singing, by becoming the god of poetry and by making close friends of the Nine Muses.

At the shrine oracles were pronounced by the woman of Delphi, the Pythia, who sat in immaculate contemplation and handed down Apollo's prophecies. Suppliants washed in the nearby cascade, paid a varying amount of money, and brought an unblemished beast, a lamb or kid goat, for sacrifice on the altar. Water from the cascade was then poured on the animal before the sacrifice: if the creature shivered (not unlikely given cold water in such heat), the omens were good. The Pythia drank water from a sacred stream over which the temple had been built, chewed the leaves of a laurel, then climbed upon the sacred tripod, laid her hand upon the *omphalos*, the stone which marked the navel of the earth, and chanted her prophecy. The *omphalos* stood at the point where the clairvoyance-giving airs were believed to emanate from the earth. The entire ritual took place on this glorious height, with the sea in the glistening distance.

Heat, even so early in the morning, made the shade of the olive groves essential and blessed. Of Italy the light is what you remember, in Greece, the smell – oregano, olive, dusty myrtle trees, giving off a spicy, dry must. Sweat pouring from my forehead pooled inside the dark lenses of my spectacles. On my left I passed a beautiful small temple, the reconstructed Treasury of the Athenians. Tall columns stood ahead in a ruined row, a giant's rubble lay strewn around, fragments of columns with fluted cores and elegant pediments. More columns made of enormous roundels, thick biscuits of white-gold stone, stood inside the high sloping ramp which opened the way into the ancient temple: did they come afresh with the reconstructed temple of 330 BC, or from the one built in 510 BC and ruined in an earthquake in 373? The first temple, they say, had been made of laurel, the next of beeswax and feathers, the third of bronze and the fourth of this local stone in 650 BC. Inside, carved inscriptions, such as the famous 'Know Thyself' and 'Nothing to Excess', stimulated reflection.

The entrance hall of the museum has a replica of the *omphalos*; it resembles a huge stone thimble, across whose surface has been criss-crossed like an embossed lattice woollen weave. Friezes and shields, depicting quarrels and heroics, battles and chases, fill other rooms. Zeus raping Europa, gods meeting on Olympus, Apollo threatening Heracles – these works, from the five or six centuries before Christ, make this museum an album of classical mythology. The stone Sphinx of Naxos, perched on her column, her wings flying, possesses a dauntless magic. The silver bull, the horse's leg, anatomically perfect, the impertinent, patronizing head of a goddess in gold and ivory, the beaten gold griffin – they have a quality, a particular unity in their demeanour which must come from their common purpose, the worship of Apollo. Along one wall stands an extraordinary series of polished stones marked with hundreds and hundreds of small hieroglyphic engravings. These are now believed to be musical notations of hymns to Apollo – Greek sheet music, as it were, carved on stone, dated to several centuries before Christ.

The entire museum has been oriented to lead the visitor to one final point, the room of the Charioteer. This bronze statue, damaged and buried in the earthquake of 373 BC, has long been regarded as one of the world's great artistic masterpieces. It depicts a young charioteer, not more than twenty years old and about six feet tall, wearing a robe flowing in folds above and below a belt, holding in his hands the reins of four horses. It formed part of a large sculptured group commissioned by the winner of the chariot races at Delphi in 478 or 474 BC. His curly hair clings to his perspiring temples, round which he wears the slender headband awarded to the winner, and his eyes, made of white enamel and brown stone, transfix whatever he sees. He would be recognized if he walked into a room today, a tough and brilliant young aristocrat, with strong hands and arms and an athlete's balance.

I stayed that night in the worst hotel in Piraeus, the port which services the anticlimactic city of Athens. Delphi proved exhausting, spiritually and physically, with the heat around 110 degrees Fahrenheit. The police advised people to stay indoors: old people, they told me, had died out on the islands in the last heat wave. Like animals feeding, and just as numerous, the ferries lined up at the port in Piraeus. I had travelled across corn-filled hills through Thivas, site of Thebes: rustic wooden signs advertised the pathway to the birthplace of Oedipus. That such insignificant places should have had such monuments, such immortalization.

The decline of the great Hellenistic period which lit the Eastern world politically and intellectually for several centuries before Christ began at the same time as the reduction of Delphi's political influence, when jurisdiction over the shrine came into the hands of the Romans. In the second century BC, as the Empire expanded, the Romans had divided the defeated Macedonian territories into four independent republics and tried unsuccessfully to introduce the 'client kingdom' principle they practised elsewhere, in which conquered countries had 'freedom' but remained dependent on Rome and were obliged to supply the Empire. (When a similar relationship in Britain came adrift on broken promises, it provoked Boadicea's rebellion.) The Greeks mistook the client relationship for a greater liberty than the Romans had intended. Brutally, the Romans then annexed Greece completely, built a Roman road into Macedonia and to cement the subjection destroyed the old southern symbolic citadel of Corinth in 146 BC.

The fourth-century Haghia Eirene, Aya Irini Kilisesi, the church of
Divine Peace. Built on the site of a temple of Aphrodite, now on
the edge of the Topkapi Palace, Haghia Eirene has become a
museum and is also used as a concert hall.

Ivory relief from the late fifth century, showing an unidentified
emperor of Constantinople, possibly Anastasius.

The Archangel Michael: this sixth-century ivory panel shows him
holding a sceptre or staff, and an orb, as a sign of his regard for the
emperor. The inscription reads: 'Receive These Gifts.' The facial
characteristics of the emperor were sometimes given to the
subjects of such cult worship.

Sixth-century mosaic of a Gothic chieftain defeated by the
Byzantine emperor. Justinian's two superb generals, Belisarius and
Narses, reclaimed those western and African territories which the
Roman Empire had lost, including Ravenna from the Goths.

Mosaic from the Imperial Palace in Istanbul, depicting a woman
with a pitcher, *c.* sixth century.

Sixth-century ivory relief of a procession taking a reliquary
to a church.

The columns at Haghia Sophia, Ayasofia, the Great Church of the
Holy or Divine Wisdom. Justinian commissioned two architects
and mathematicians to build a church which would harmonize the
symbolic and physical powers of God and the Empire.

Interior of Haghia Sophia, lit by forty windows in the massive
dome. The high-ceilinged gallery traditionally belonged to the
women.

The Romans were already aware of Delphi: as early as the fifth century BC a Roman leader had paid tribute at the shrine in thanksgiving for a military victory. The importance of Delphi's symbolism to the Greeks could not be mistaken, and it acted as as challenge to those who wished to conquer Delphi in a local war, or Greece itself. Celts had attacked the shrine in 279 BC, but Apollo had poured rain and snow down on them, a move which greatly assisted the Aetolians who defended Delphi. A series of wars between 600 and 339 BC, during some of which the shrine's treasures were plundered to meet expenses, had shaken Delphi but none the less enhanced the lustrous reputation of the place. When the Romans took command the oracles no longer influenced the affairs of Greece with pronouncements of political importance. In 86 BC Lucius Cornelius Sulla, a Roman general besieging Athens (and in the process laying waste Piraeus) took from Delphi any valuable metals the shrine had retained in order to pay for his campaign. Three years later raiders quenched the eternal flame and caused damage to the temple. A hundred and fifty years on Nero, while professing to respect the shrine of Apollo, coveted the statues and took several hundred of them back to Rome. By the second century AD Christianity had begun to spread widely, with a consequent loss of devotion to Apollo, and though various Roman emperors acknowledged the former glory of the place, attending games and ceremonials there, and in some cases ordering restoration works on the temple, Delphi's great era had ended.

Constantine, though he had been honoured at the shrine, enhanced his new city in the East with some of Delphi's masterpieces. In 360 the Emperor Julian the Apostate, Constantine's half-brother, declared himself a pagan and attempted to restore the stature of Delphi. Finally, in 392, the devout but savage Emperor Theodosius ordered Delphi to be closed and the temple to be silenced. At the same time Greece was fully annexed into the Eastern Empire and played a substantial part in the affairs of Constantinople.

Throughout the fifth and sixth centuries the shrine of Apollo became a place of Christian worship, a bishopric, where the Christians built churches out of the stones and ancient monuments. By the end of the seventh century Delphi constituted a metaphor for Greece's fate – in ruins, overgrown, trampled upon, colonized, made to worship new gods, unimportant in the scheme of things, a yardstick of how the old pagan classical civilization had collapsed. Greece in the Dark Ages generally experienced enormous upheaval. Mass evacuation took place: the entire population of Patras may have moved across the Adriatic. Greek settlements were numerous in southern Italy, and the presence of Greeks in a community already mixed with Romans, other Italians, Goths, Jews, caused considerable problems. Greece's identity, even within the Byzantine Empire, had been eroded by

The Golden Gate, Istanbul, erected by the Emperor Theodosius.

invasions of tribespeople from the north, Slavs, Bulgars, Avars: the Empire only had effective control of the eastern shoreline of Greece down to the Peloponnese. The country did not regain any political Hellenistic *persona* of its own until the Byzantine recovery of the ninth century, and even then it had much Slavonic content.

I set out from Piraeus on a Sunday morning to reach, eventually, Istanbul. The route I had intended would take me on another long ferry journey up through the islands to Lesbos, and from there to Turkey. I walked to the harbour at half past seven down the narrow street, past the white marble steps leading up to the open door of an Orthodox church. People had begun to gather – very few, mostly old women and a child or two. Beyond the wide rows of golden icons the bearded priest chanted and was answered by a middle-aged man in a grey summer shirt who sat behind a high lectern. Though more exotic (partly because of the language) than the ceremonies of my childhood, the elements in common could be seen – the raising of the priest above the level of the worshippers, the drawing of the eye towards the light of the candles, the hypnotic calling of the prayers, the soothing yet anxious atmosphere of the icons and decorations. The notice board outside listed several services for the morning.

The boat from Piraeus to Mytilini in Lesbos was certainly bigger than the large wooden boats, like galleys or Egyptian dhows, in which travellers of the seventh century left Greece for the East. The islands that drifted in and out of this dreadfully hot noon haze must have looked exactly the same to the monk as they did to me. Pirates infested the busy seas then, greater dangers existed, he had more difficulties. I tried to work out, on this virtually empty ferry, how long the journey from Ireland would have taken him. Allow for rest periods, for times of new instruction in monasteries, for weeks or months of bad weather, for helping in a community short of workers at harvest-time, for assisting in the creation of a new manuscript, for the copying of a gospel book, for the celebration of a saint or the consecration of a bishop, for the withstanding of, or clearing up after, a raid. Allow time for ill health, or ministering to the sick after a swingeing local epidemic, or a wide diversion following the collapse of a bridge over an unfordable river, or the avoidance of a region currently known to contain especially fierce wolves or bears or brigands. His journey could have been completed in between fifteen and eighteen months, on foot, on horseback, on a cart in a convoy, on water.

He did not have time to dwell everywhere for long enough – in this he had my complete sympathy – nor could he consider everything to his full or even reasonable satisfaction, and he too must have arrived at this golden bowl of the world, the land of islands, with his head full of a wild and varied kaleidoscope to which were now added the colours of Lesbos. Sappho lived in this 'pleasant grove of apple trees, and altars fragrant with frankincense; there, cold water babbles among apple branches, all the place is shaded with roses, sleep comes down from the trembling leaves. There is a meadow for

horses, blossoming with spring flowers, and gentle breezes blow ... .'
Sappho hung her lyre upon the temple of Apollo and jumped from a cliff,
supposedly to her death, but on the way down she was changed into a swan
and flew away over the Aegean: 'I love delicacy, and the bright and
beautiful belong for me to the desire of the sunlight.'

Birthplace of Aesop of the Fables, setting for *Daphnis and Chloe*, Lesbos
has wooded roads, olives and myrtle and big grey birds. It also has a
typically long, typically chequered history. Thucydides, the Athenian
historian of the Peloponnese Wars, told how the inhabitants of Lesbos
turned their coats and reneged upon the Athenians in favour of the
Spartans. A galley, bearing death-dealing soldiers, sailed for the island
under instructions to execute each and every islander citizen, but another
galley, also from Athens, performing one of the greatest feats of rowing,
brought news of a reprieve just as the announcement of the carnage-to-be
was being promulgated. In Mytilini people were quick to point out that
Turkey lay only just across the way. Ancient enemies, ancient fears that the
Turks might one day again cast eyes of desire upon Lesbos, island of the
petrified forest and the richest greenery in the archipelago, 'where the
nightingales sing more sweetly than anywhere else', and where the women,
according to Homer, 'won the chief renown for beauty from their whole
fair sex'.

❖

Say Istanbul and a seagull comes to mind
Half silver and half foam, half fish and half bird.
Say Istanbul and a fable comes to mind
The old wives' tale that we have all heard.

Say Istanbul and mottled grapes come to mind
With three candles burning bright on the basket –
Suddenly along comes a girl so ruthlessly female

So lovely to look at that you gasp,
Her lips ripe with grape honey,
A girl luscious and lustful from top to toe –
Southern wind, willow branch, the dance of joy ....

Thus wrote the poet Bedri Rahmi Eynboglu in 'The Sign of Istanbul'.

Begin with the name, and the name began with Byzantium, after Byzas son of Poseidon and grandson of Zeus. His grandmother, Io, another mistress of Zeus, had, like Apollo's mother, to flee the jealous anger of Hera, Zeus's wife, who turned Io into a heifer and let loose upon her a stinging fly. Io plunged into the waters, which since then have been called Bosphorus, the ford of the cow. More practically, but with some mythical input, the city was founded on the geographical instruction of the oracle at Delphi, who told Greek colonists from near Corinth where to build. This happened in 658 BC, and three centuries later the symbol with which the city is most synonymous, the crescent moon, became the immortal emblem of this eastern region, and eventually of Islam. Philip the Macedonian attacked Byzantium in a surprise midnight raid. The Byzantines prayed to the goddess of the moon and she took away her light, leaving only a sliver, not enough by which to mount a successful attack. Afterwards they promised to remember the goddess forever in their banners.

Exhausted, I arrived at night, filthy, with several days' growth of salt-and-pepper beard. The hotel queried, then discouraged, my reservation, made several weeks before – almost the only advance booking I had made anywhere on this journey; the receptionist, otherwise pleasant, asked me for proof of identity, then to confirm my payment. When the air conditioning of the lift hit me my clothes adhered all over. The word 'manky', forgotten since schooldays, returned; I stank, high – clothes 'manky' with sweat stains. On days of temperatures just above the hundred mark I had spent too many hours in buses from beyond Izmir, travelling ovens, at a steady forty miles an hour. In Mytilini, the midnight temperature still skulked in the eighties and the unthinkable happened in front of my eyes – elderly Greek women, come out to dine with their families, actually took off their woollen cardigans.

The morning light over the Golden Horn seemed to reveal the curve of the earth, an illusion caused by the way in which, through the slightly bending glass of the window, the heat haze of the distance, a kind of grey-purple, cut off the view across the crowded hills. Roofs everywhere, in ragged plateaus; the colours of the tiles, many in disrepair, ranged from cinnamon and deeper terracotta to bright red; one long eave had been patched with a wide stripe of brilliant blue plastic, and from the shadows of the houses at street level occasional doors of turquoise or green or white perked up the rickety neighbourhood. Through the other window the Bosphorus became as busy as the life of a pond, ferries and pilot boats and tugs, ushering and shoving, back and forth.

My face lifted with the peeling skin, and the breeze rushing into the room stung my forehead. I will remember every hot, abusive inch of the Dardanelles for the rest of my life – and the grubbiness of Athens and the

Greek fire, the secret weapon of the Byzantine navy.

crestfallen disappointment in Troy. It now consists of no more than some badly restored walls, a hideous replica of the Wooden Horse, and some unremarkable earthen mounds, slopes of browned grass, which lack the force of the hillforts in Ireland or Argyll. I discovered one thing with clarity: the introspection experienced while travelling, especially during great heat, has a different quality from that of the everyday kind, and more frequently – or perhaps I mean more rapidly – the introspection becomes depression, becomes despair. Followed by that sneak thief, that con man, elation.

A smell of coffee niggled in from somewhere – not the cliché of the Turkish bazaar, this coffee was being brewed nearby, in some service room of the hotel. Such a jostling place, Istanbul. The formal lustre of Byzantium has given way to the shabby hustle of the grey city. The notion of those immediate golden backgrounds on which the icons and mosaics were painted, those dignified and brilliant images, was straightaway overwhelmed by traffic and German industry and fumes, heavy fumes, enough to make you cough, from too many engines. Istanbul has not yet travelled far enough around its own circle to be able to afford to burnish the past that was Byzantium and Constantinople. The entrances to the museums and castles had the shabbiness of such barely necessary amenities in all poor cities – other requirements, more urgent than history, must take precedence.

The heat of the morning continued to enter through the open window. No breeze, no pasha's fan turning overhead. My arms were sore, my neck and my forehead raw. When the citizens here had to defend their city against the Arabs in a four-year siege during the seventh century, they made use of an old Greek invention, a Byzantine cocktail called Greek Fire, a mixture of lime, sulphur, perhaps a little mustard and saltpetre, and some liquid with the properties of paraffin or petrol. When hurled, even on water, it burst into flames. Some of it must still be hanging about the place, if my face offers anything to go by. I supposed it could well be raining now on Skellig Michael.

Out in the air a chanting to prayer dinned across, above the roofs. I had never heard it before, a sound both cranky and arrogant, and it brought with it another disappointment – the minarets had posies of loudspeakers clustered to them, the sound had a metallic quality. Perhaps they use recordings, like poor parishes of the Church of England. 'And the silken girls bringing sherbet' – I remembered fragments from Eliot's 'The Journey of the Magi' as I walked down the street to the hotel. The road I came in along had cobbles for miles, perhaps the only cobbled motorway in the world.

> And the cities hostile and the towns unfriendly,
> And the villages dirty and charging high prices.

Byzantium; Constantinople; Stamboul; Istanbul. 'O City, Chief of all Cities, City Centre of all Parts of the World! O City! City, the glory of

Christians, and confusion of barbarians! O City, City second Paradise planted in the West with every tree abundant in its spiritual fruits! Paradise where is your beauty? Where is that copious outpouring of graces so salutary for body and soul?' Few cities in the world have been so assaulted, few cities have been so worth assaulting, few cities have been so dramatically lamented by their historians, such as – in this case – Michael Ducas. To the western colonists, Byzantium's location seemed like the door of a treasure-house called the East and vice versa, and thus the battles raged, for a thousand years since Byzas's foundation until Constantine, on 11 May, AD 330, formally inaugurated the New Rome, Constantinople.

Constantine had come from the Roman patrician classes who saw Christianity as no more than a creed followed by artisans, plebs, foreigners and slaves – yet he had been converted. On an October day in 312, as he prepared for a final battle against Maxentius, a rival contender for the position of emperor after the abdication and retirement of Diocletian, a cross of sunlight appeared in the sky, bearing the instruction, 'In this Sign Conquer'. He put the sign of the cross on his banners and did conquer, and took control, an impulsive man of great energy and self-confidence, a man in whom the civil administrator and military commander combined to create the empire builder. He had travelled throughout the Empire and had often lived outside Rome – it was at York, remember, that his soldiers acclaimed him Emperor – and he decided that the frontiers of the Empire, both in the Rhine and Danube valleys, and, to the east, along the Euphrates could better be supervised from a more strategically placed city than Rome. He measured the extent of his New Rome by walking: Edward Gibbon, in his *Decline and Fall of the Roman Empire*, describes Constantine's dream the night before (or rather, how later writers interpreted what Constantine might have seen):

The tutelar genius of the city, a venerable matron sinking under the weight of years and infirmities, was suddenly transformed into a blooming maid, whom his own hands adorned with all the symbols of Imperial greatness. The monarch awoke, interpreted the auspicious omen, and obeyed, without hesitation, the will of Heaven .... On foot, with a lance in his hand, the emperor himself led the solemn procession, and directed the line which was traced as the boundary of the destined capital, till the growing circumference was observed with astonishment by the assistants who, at length, ventured to observe that he had already exceeded the most ample measure of a great city.

At which point Constantine made it plain to his companions that the initial survey of the site lay in the hands of another – 'HE, the invisible guide who marches before me . . . .'

With intense industry, the Emperor then built a city of memorable style. 'A particular description,' wrote Gibbon,

composed a century after its foundation, enumerates a capitol or school of learning, a circus, two theatres, eight public and one hundred and fifty-three private baths, fifty-two porticoes, five granaries, eight aqueducts or reservoirs of water, four spacious halls for the meetings of the senate or courts of justice, fourteen churches, fourteen palaces, and four thousand, three hundred and eighty-eight houses which, for their size or beauty, deserved to be distinguished from the multitude of plebeian habitations.

This, the New or Second Rome, became a byword both for splendour and for efficient administration. The man who presided over it was described by Gibbon:

His stature was lofty, his countenance majestic, his deportment graceful; his strength and activity were displayed in every manly exercise, and, from his earliest youth to a very advanced season of life, he preserved the vigour of his constitution by a strict adherence to the domestic virtues of chastity and temperance. He delighted in the social intercourse of familiar conversation; and though he might sometimes indulge his disposition to raillery with less reserve than was required by the severe dignity of his station, the courtesy and liberality of his manners gained the hearts of all who approached him.

He also had his own son, Crispus, of whom he was jealous, executed. Constantine died in 337 at the age of sixty-four, at Nicomedia, appropriately at the noontide of Pentecost. His body was drawn slowly to his city in a gold coffin and his name stayed as his monument until the city fell to the Ottoman Empire, who even then called it Konstantinye, and eventually Stamboul, Istanbul.

Two centuries after Constantine died, when Justinian became Emperor, the city's population stood at about three-quarters of a cosmopolitan million. Constantinople represented a confluence of East and West. Under Justinian Germanic cavalry had honour in the ranks of the Empire's soldiery, part of the military and social fabric, here as in Italy. Copts from Egypt, people from Illyria and various tribal regions along the east coast of the Adriatic, Hittites and Armenians and Jews and Syrians and Italians and Greeks and Goths – they teemed in a city that could be a tinder box when it came to civil disagreement, a city notorious for major riots, quelled with equally notorious ferocity. A high level of employment existed, due principally to the bureaucratic infrastructure of the administration, where, confusingly, Latin prevailed. The support industries throve too, with accountants, jewellers, weavers, carpenters and a host of other trades. The tradesmen belonged to guilds, which regulated prices and apprenticeships – admissions to trades came under strict scrutiny.

The diet consisted of meat, often pork, fish, beans, barley, bread, wine, shellfish. Wheat became scarce after the granaries of Egypt were lost to Islam. The control of the food supply became one of the most important public functions. Most citizens received a measure of free food, principally bread – not out of altruism, but because in an environment where the supply of raw materials could be volatile hunger caused riots quicker than politics did. Beggars slept in the alleyways in the interstices of the houses; fires broke out frequently and destroyed entire streets. The wealthy travelled on horseback or in closed carriages, always protected against robbers. The common people walked everywhere – even nowadays the streets and lanes and bridges of Istanbul become so crowded that pushing through them feels like being part of a permanent football crowd. And still the street vendors try to lure you into their booths, to buy handmade leather which they tool before your eyes, and still they sell to all on the street food from instant stalls which unfold from bicycles, or kittens or small goats which they carry inside their jackets, or little donkey foals, or jewellery.

Justinian waited in the wings until his uncle, the elderly Justin, died in 527. While being patient he cultivated cliques of support, including a section of the populace known as the Blues, whose membership was led by wealthy conservatives and whose rivals, the Greens, hooting at them in the Hippodrome or at the games, or in the street riots, consisted of merchants and tradesmen. Justinian used his power to excess, and brutally, in favour of the Blues, who carried on rackets of blackmail, robbery and murder. In their company he met the woman who joined in his fame as he set out to establish a reputation as the brilliant ruler and entrepreneur of an Empire which once again, though briefly, became as dazzling as Rome had ever been.

The Byzantine historian Procopius, who was Belisarius's secretary, had a waspish and bitter demeanour in his writing. He also vacillated – across three sets of works his opinions of the Emperor and the Empress varied. In his *Historiae* – of Justinian's Gothic, Vandal and Persian wars – he adopted a neutral, factual position. In *De Aedificiis*, his discussion of the public buildings of the Empire, he became complimentary. He wrote a third book, however, *Historia Arcana*, the Secret History, in which he said he put facts unsuited to the disciplines of his other works: in short, he wrote a scandalous account of the lives and times of his Emperor and Empress.

He described Justinian's Empress, Theodora, the 'actress' daughter of a bear-keeper, in the following terms:

Before Theodora remained developed to the point where she could please a man in bed, or enjoy full womanly sexual activity, she acted like a young male prostitute, attracting clients of a very low sort, even slaves .... When she was old enough, though, she became a full-blooded courtesan ... and sold her total bodily pleasures to all and sundry. She did not possess even the smallest jot of modesty, and responded eagerly to the most lascivious requests ... quite capable of throwing off all her clothes and showing off those parts of her, before and behind, which common decency requires to be concealed from men's eyes .... She used to tease her clients, she made them wait, and then experimented with new methods of making love ... she went to parties with ten companions, copulated with each one, and then with their servants, often more than thirty in a night .... In the theatre she took off all her clothes except the compulsory girdle and lay face upward, her legs spread wide apart. Her servant then sprinkled barley grains upon her intimate parts and geese, trained specially, picked the grains off one by one.

Justinian married her in his early forties, and he had to change the laws of the Empire – which decreed that no member of the ruling body could marry somebody who appeared on the stage – in order to make Theodora his Empress. They married in the huge church of Haghia Sophia, where large black and gold discs bearing symbols of Islam now hang over the central concourse in the greatest basilica of the Byzantine world, originated by Constantine two hundred years before, and then rebuilt by Justinian.

Justinian's two superb generals, Belisarius and Narses, reclaimed for a time those Italian and African territories which the Roman Empire had lost to the Goths and Vandals. With his learned advisers Justinian drafted and redrafted laws for all citizens of the Empire, terrorized the Pope and pronounced on matters of Church as well as State. His lady wife Theodora, who had once reproached nature for not giving her a further orifice at her breast – 'to accommodate', as Gibbon put it, 'another dart, she wished for a fourth altar on which to pour her libations of love' – continued to lead a licentious existence in the palace surrounded by eunuchs and friends, while in his public statements her husband raised her to the level of living sainthood.

Justinian and Theodora both appear as semi-divine in the mosaics at Ravenna. During their reign, Halley's Comet passed across the skies and earthquakes shook Constantinople, in one instance for forty successive days. A plague came in from Syria and Persia, obviously of the kind that, as described by Paul the Deacon, had infected Lombard northern Italy in 566 and, according to Gregory of Tours, parts of France in 580. Gibbon describes similar symptoms: 'The infection was sometimes announced by the visions of a distempered fancy, and the victim despaired as soon as he had heard the menace and felt the stroke of an invisible spectre.' Eventually, as the illness progressed, 'The fever was often accompanied with lethargy or delirium; the bodies of the sick were covered with black pustules or carbuncles, the symptoms of immediate death.' Five to ten thousand people a day died in Constantinople, a savage toll, in that plague. Gibbon, perhaps too harshly, sums up Justinian's reign, the one whose imprint remained the most vivid in the time of our monk, as follows: 'The triple scourge of war, pestilence and famine afflicted the subjects of Justinian, and his reign is disgraced by a visible decrease of the human species which has never been repaired in some of the fairest countries of the globe.'

Theodora died on 28 June 548. Her husband died seventeen years later on 14 November 565. Some would say that at this point the Fall of Constantinople, not completed until 1453, had begun. By 687 the city had increasingly come under extreme pressure from internecine revolt and external threat. Two years before the monk arrived, in 685, Justinian II had ascended the throne, an ill man. By that time all the gains Justinian had made 160 years earlier had been lost. A period of long dynastic rulerships had, however, followed Justinian I, in which the remarkable Heraclius almost outshone both Constantine and Justinian.

With various hiccups, four emperors succeeded Justinian before Heraclius – Justin II, then Tiberius 578–82, Maurice 582–602 and Phocas 602–10 – an appalling, drunken, red-haired despot who had his predecessor assassinated. Heraclius, son of the Exarch of Carthage, was sent for by the patricians of Constantinople. The Frankish historian Fredegar described him as 'striking in appearance, for he was handsome, tall, braver than others and a great fighter. He would often kill lions in the arena and many a wild boar in unfrequented places. Being well read he practised astrology by

Coin of the reign of Justinian II.

which art he discovered, God helping him, that his empire would be laid waste by circumcised races' – an omen which led him to sanction a massacre of Jews in 629, unaware that the equally circumcised Arabs were to be the real downfall of the Empire. Heraclius invaded Constantinople with a fleet, tortured and decapitated Phocas and, upon becoming Emperor, immediately had to deal with the Persians in a war that had begun four years earlier in 606 and was to last until 628. In the end Heraclius defeated the Persians and recovered the lost territories of Syria and Egypt. But since the Empire had been debilitated by the length and ferocity of the Persian wars it lay feeble before the ominously emerging Arab powers that captured Damascus in 635, only three years after the death of Islam's founder, Mohammed.

This new force, fast, lethal and inspired, rocketing like a phenomenon out of the desert, impinged hugely upon the life of Constantinople in 687–8. The march of the Arab world brought Mohammed's followers into north-west Africa by the middle of the century, poised for southern Europe. After conquering Syria and laying siege unsuccessfully to Constantinople from 674 to 678 they came back in 717 and were repelled once more. And so it was to go on, a long, lingering death, with brief periods of remission, until the end came in 1453.

Once it held the title of Second Paradise and was called Mistress of the World, a strategic connotation. Istanbul offers not an end to a journey, but a starting point: you need to live here, not visit. The population stands at nearly seven million, many of them piled high in apartments, or in shanty towns behind great streets. The taxi driver took me up narrow streets to meet his friends, hectic alleys where the people had no visible means of support. Winding untarred lanes, some quite wide, lined with tilting houses of old wooden construction shored up with galvanized iron, contained dark-eyed children and men who stood on the street and talked, and women who sat. The city seemed unbalanced, toppled over by the poor, a city of small traders and old cars with rattling exhausts.

The Column of Constantine, the ruins of which still stand near the old bazaar, once housed in its base a time capsule chosen from the best of the Old and the New Testaments – the axe with which Noah built the Ark, the stone from which Moses drew water when he struck it with his staff, the loaves of bread from the Wedding at Cana where Christ turned the water into wine (though some said they came from the Miracle of the Loaves and Fishes, where a lot had been left over), and the alabaster ointment box which Mary Magdalene used when bathing the feet of Christ.

Haghia Sophia, the Great Church of the Holy Wisdom, stands out clear and calm among the mosques and minarets on the hill across the Golden

Horn. By the time my Irish pilgrim arrived here the Christianity of western Europe had just launched its Golden Age, while at the very gates of Constantinople Islam had begun to preside over its ruthless decline in the East. The Christian territories beyond Constantinople, once the most devout of all the regions of Christianity, when conquered by Islam were never regained.

'Now above these arches is raised a circular building of a curved form through which the light of day first shines, for the building which I imagine overtops the whole country, has small openings left on purpose, so that the places where these intervals occur may serve for the light to come through. Thus far I imagine the building is not capable of being described, even by a weak and feeble tongue.' Procopius had difficulty in grasping and then conveying in mere language the generous austerity of Haghia Sophia. The warm walls with pillars rise far to Heaven; the mosaics and decoration, where they can still be seen, and the general traces of Justinian's Empire and Constantine's intent have exhausted the efforts of centuries of writers and invaders. The difficulty in perceiving the building today lies in the fact that, though granted the status of a museum, it none the less feels like a temple in which the gods are confused. It may once have seen the coronations of emperors, and was raised in order to sing the glory of the Christian God, and then echoed to the wailed glories of Allah and dignified submission to Him embodied in the word Islam – but it fell to invaders in circumstances throughout which political and territorial considerations received a spiritual dimension. The spiritual connection which the building's architecture was intended to make has therefore been deflected, and, though gorgeous to inspect, the mix of religion and politics promoted unease in me. At least in Ayasofia (as it is now called) this discomfort can, presumably, be overcome by a concentration upon the architectural details.

The light pours in through forty windows in the massive dome which measures 101 feet in diameter and 180 feet in height; the church, 345 feet long, has two smaller domes east and west. The gallery, high-ceilinged and spacious, traditionally belonged to the women – except for one section reserved for the imperial household and for religious and theological councils. Eight of the huge marble columns which stalk the nave had been taken from an early Constantinople building – the materials for others were quarried on an island in the Sea of Marmara. In the vestibule, protected by enormous doors of bronze reminiscent of the Pantheon's doors, though lighter in tone and structure, the tenth-century mosaics need much light to be inspected fully. When revealed they show an idealized Mother and Christ flanked by Constantine offering a model of Constantinople and an unusually humble Justinian offering a model of Haghia Sophia; he wears the crossed vestments of a priest, has a halo and strapped sandals. The motif of a prelate or secular dignitary offering the building or city over which they had jurisdiction recurs throughout the imagery of the Byzantines – creating both an impression of the power held by the incumbent and the greater power of God and His Mother which the temporal leader acknowledges, as well as the semi-divine stature of the ruler.

On a more accessible scale Haghia Eirene, Aya Irini Kilisesi, the Church of Divine Peace, built in 300, on the site of a temple to Aphrodite, now on the edge of the Topkapi Palace, has become a museum and is also used as a concert hall. It has a sweetness in its nature and size, and in the Byzantine-ness of its scale and humour – smaller though in the same harmonies as Haghia Sophia, pillars and arches walking towards an altar in the distance, a domed peace with a gallery and dry walls, and dry air. Although it has experienced many rebuildings – as a result of earthquakes and fires – and the oldest visible parts date to the sixth century, it echoes the compact and organized round, domed buildings of classical Byzantine architecture as portrayed in the mosaics at Ravenna. The interior, quiet, cool and lofty, has three aisles with colannades and large columns supporting the central dome.

Resisting the blandishments of the rug sellers and the jewellers became an exhausting matter; on the one occasion on which I succumbed, certain that what I had agreed to would turn out to be spurious, I received a brilliant surprise. Unlike the larger museums around the Topkapi which possess many Babylonian artefacts, and boast a bust of Alexander as well as his sarcophagus, the Mosaic Museum does not seem like a building that has official saction. Down a modernized arcade, where the windows offer hookahs and the ineluctable Turkish carpets, the museum advertises itself with a brass plaque and very little authority. Inside, though unattractively laid out, in a loose collection of rooms, fragments of mosaic, many from the Great Palace, bid to become the most vivid I have yet seen, Ravenna notwithstanding. Stronger, more muscularly built and decorated, their colours do not gleam so lustrously as those at Ravenna or Haghia Sophia, yet – probably because they were designed as pavements for everyday use rather than precious exhibitions of spiritual high-mindedness and worship – they oddly open a pathway into a more tangible world.

The pictures include animals slaughtering and being slaughtered, heroes

Mosaic from the Great Palace of Constantinople.

in fights against villains or beasts, foliage, wooded environments, scenes from mythology. The combination of artist and artisan emerges strongly; these mosaicists built their work to last despite extensive use, and their tesserae were made of hard minerals. In Ravenna and in other civilizations, mosaicists included chips of gold, silver and more delicate substances such as the scales of reptiles and glass paste which they coloured as required. On these Byzantine pavements, dated to the fourth and fifth centuries, they used onyx, marble, green serpentine, mother of pearl, quartz, and rocks coloured with natural minerals, all beautiful and beautifully distributed, but above all durable. The mosaicists had substantial artistic talent; the anatomical accuracy and the life drawing of the animals and humans is exciting and universal: seen fifteen centuries later, their creations maintain total continuity – the figures, whether animal or human, and the flora are immediately recognizable.

Outside, not far away, a tiny shop in a busy street was crammed from top to bottom, in every corner and open piece of space, whether floor or counter, with spices – in sticks, powders, seeds, lumps, in boxes, jars and old brown paper bags of a kind which disappeared from western Europe twenty years ago. The proprietor sold vanilla pods, seed pods of cardamom, and saffron taken from the stamens of the orange-gold crocus. He and the other clichés of Istanbul and Turkey that I had seen and bewilderedly tried to encompass in a few days hammered home a point that Edward Gibbon made in his notes to the second edition of his *Decline and Fall of the Roman Empire*: 'The distinction of North and South is real and intelligible; the difference between East and West is arbitrary and shifts around the globe.' Not for a moment did I feel easy in Istanbul – I suspect that I should have found the seventh-century city easier to adjust to and comprehend. My head filled with staccato reverberations: too many people, the fervour of the devout at the mosques, too overstated for me, like the Christians praying aloud on the ferry back from Iona – and then the contrasts: the elegant linen coat worn by well-to-do gentlemen and called a Stamboul or a Stambouline, the endless supplications of peddlers and beggars, the beautifully gowned wives and the maimed. The city denies, crowds out the thinking function; only the sensation function can be made to work. I felt guilty about leaving my monk standing here, even in his time, fearing foolishly that he must have been as uneasy at the gates of the East of his day as I now felt. Still, if he discovered nothing else, he realized that the small island patch from which he had come did not constitute the centre of the universe, did not command the high moral ground of the world, did not hold the key to mankind's spirit. And he collided with a profound irony, since the word 'Islam' means 'resignation', or 'submission' – that is to say, submission to the will of God, and in the late seventh century Christianity and the cities which had constituted its most holy tabernacles outside of

Rome seemed about to submit, not to the will of God, but to submission itself, to Islam.

He stood on the edge of his past, in the Empire commanding the deserts of the anchorite fathers. South of the Mareotic Lake, round which the sages spake, in Nitria at the edge of deserts which stretched to Ethiopia, they had lived as he did on the Skelligs, in huts of stone, with a reed mat for a bed, a reed stool which at night became a pillow, drinking only water, eating their rough bread. There was God, if you like. 'Remember,' said Bede, 'I am but dust and wind and shadow and life as fleeting as the flowers of grass. But may the eternal mercy which hath shone from time of old rescue Thy servant from the jaws of the lion.'

The full circle of time and the imagination: I had set out to travel in the footsteps of such a man, not to make a comparative study of Europe then and now – too vast a subject, and already catered for excellently elsewhere. I had wanted to make a long journey which would link for me the pastoral ease and rich oral heritage of Ireland with the excitement and complexity of those civilizations of the Mediterranean and the Near East. The man who travelled from Skellig Michael to the gates of the East made a brief and illuminating passage out of some kind of darkness and into some kind of light. He wandered away from the traps of parochial and insular experience into a wider world, out of the residual darkness of childhood into a time of learning – and as with all such processes there was no digestion as yet of what he had learned.

I still had Bede in my bag, the *Ecclesiastical History of the English Nation*, and read him with kebabs and crumbling cheese in a huge restaurant, surrounded by more poor people than I had ever seen in one room. In the early seventh century Bishop Paulinus of York, whom Bede described as 'a tall man, a little stooping, with black hair, a meagre visage and a slender aquiline nose, with a presence venerable and awe-inspiring', preached to Edwin, the King of Northumbria, and his assembled soldiers. As he rose to full evangelical powers, a bird flew through the hall. One of Edwin's 'chief men' observed,

The present life of man, O King, seems to me, in comparison of that time which is unknown to us, like to the swift flight of a sparrow through the room where you sit at supper in winter, with your commanders and ministers, and a good fire in the midst, whilst the storms of rain and snow prevail abroad; the sparrow, I say, flying in at one door, and immediately out at another, whilst he is within, is safe from the wintry storm; but after that short space of fair weather, he immediately vanishes out of sight, out into the dark weather from which he had emerged. So, the life of man appears for a short space. But of what went before, or what is to follow, we are utterly ignorant.

His words could have applied to all the *peregrinii*, hardbitten or dying by the way, turning their faces back to home or permanently exiled.

SELECT BIBLIOGRAPHY

BEDE, ed. J. A. Giles: *Ecclesiastical History of the English Nation*. George Bell, London, 1900.

BROWN, PETER: *Society and the Holy in Late Antiquity*. Faber, London, 1982.

BROWNING, ROBERT: *Justinian and Theodora*. Weidenfeld and Nicolson, London, 1971.

BRUNDAGE, JAMES A.: *Law, Sex and Christian Society in Medieval Europe*. University of Chicago Press, Chicago and London, 1987.

CAMPBELL, JOSEPH: *Papers from the Eranos Yearbooks*, Bollingen Series XXX. Pantheon Books and Bollingen Foundation, New York, 1955.

FINLEY, M. I.: *Economy and Society in Ancient Greece*. Chatto and Windus, London, 1971.

FREDEGAR, trans. J. M. Wallace-Hadrill, *The Fourth Book of the Chronicle of Fredegar*. Thomas Nelson and Sons, London, 1960.

DUCAS, MICHAEL, *The History of the Emperors John Manuel, John and Constantine Paleologus*, Bucharest, 1948.

GIBBON, EDWARD: *The History of the Decline and Fall of the Roman Empire*. The Folio Society, London, 1984-7.

GREGORY OF TOURS, trans. Lewis Thorpe: *The History of the Franks*. Penguin, London, 1986.

JAMES, EDWARD: *The Origins of France*. Macmillan, London, 1982.

JOHNSON, PAUL: *A History of Christianity*. Weidenfeld and Nicolson, London, 1976.

JOHNSON, PAUL: *A History of the Jews*. Weidenfeld and Nicolson, London, 1987.

LEVI, PETER: *The Frontiers of Paradise*. Collins Harvill, London, 1987.

LLEWELLYN, PETER: *Rome in the Dark Ages*. Faber, London, 1971.

MACAIRT, SEAN, ed.: *The Annals of Innisfallen*. Dublin Institute for Advanced Studies, 1951.

MCNEILL, WILLIAM: *Plagues and Peoples*. Blackwell, Oxford, 1977.

MOORHOUSE, GEOFFREY: *Against All Reason*. Weidenfeld and Nicolson, London, 1969.

NEILL, STEPHEN: *A History of Christian Missions*. Pelican, London, 1986.

PARKE, H. W.: *Festivals of the Athenians*. Thames and Hudson, London, 1977.

PAULUS DEACONUS, trans. William Dudley Foulke: *History of the Langobards*. University of Pennsylvania, Philadelphia, and Longmans, London, 1907.

PAUSANIUS, trans. Peter Levi: *Guide to Greece*. Penguin Books, London, 1971.

RICHE, PIERRE, trans. Jo Ann McNamara: *Daily Life in the World of Charlemagne*. Liverpool University Press, 1978.

SARTON, GEORGE: *Ancient and Modern Civilisation*. Edward Arnold, London, and Nebraska University Press, 1954.

STOKES, GEORGE T. and Hugh Jackson Lawlor: *Ireland and the Celtic Church*. Macmillan, London, 1928.

THOMAS, CHARLES: *Christianity in Roman Britain to AD 500*. Batsford, London, 1981.

THOMAS, CHARLES: *Celtic Britain*. Thames and Hudson, London, 1986.

WADDELL, HELEN: *Songs of the Wandering Scholars*. The Folio Society, London, 1982.

WADDELL, HELEN: *The Desert Fathers*. Constable, London, 1936 and 1987.

WEBB, J. F., ed.: *The Age of Bede*. Penguin, London, 1986.

PHOTOGRAPHIC
ACKNOWLEDGEMENTS

COLOUR INSERT ONE

Page 33, Des Lavelle; 34 *above*, Des Lavelle; 34 *below*, Ancient Monuments Section, Board of Works, Dublin; 35, Bord Failte Eireann; 36, The Board of Trinity College Dublin; 37, National Museum of Ireland; 38 *above*, David Paterson; 38 *below*, Ted Spiegel/Susan Griggs Agency; 39, Michael Holford; 40, The British Library.

COLOUR INSERT TWO

Page 73, Charlie Waite/Landscape Only; 74, Ronald Sheridan's Photo Library; 75, Ronald Sheridan's Photo Library; 76, Ronald Sheridan's Photo Library; 77, Bridgeman Art Library; 78, Stiftsbibliothek, St Gallen; 79, Stiftsbibliothek, St Gallen; 80, Horst Munzig/Susan Griggs Agency.

COLOUR INSERT THREE

Page 113, Scala, Florence; 114, *above*, Giraudon, Paris; 114 *below*, Giraudon, Paris; 115, Scala, Florence; 116, Scala, Florence; 117, Erich Lessing/John Hillelson Agency; 118, Sonia Halliday Photographs; 119, Michael Holford; 120, Scala, Florence.

COLOUR INSERT FOUR

Page 169, Erich Lessing/John Hillelson Agency; 170, Scala, Florence; 171, Sonia Halliday Photographs; 172, Werner Forman Archive; 173, Werner Forman Archive; 174, Scala, Florence; 175, Erich Lessing/John Hillelson Agency; 176, Landscape Only.

COLOUR INSERT FIVE

Page 209, Sonia Halliday Photographs; 210, Ronald Sheridan's Photo Library; 211, Michael Holford; 212, Sonia Halliday Photographs; 213, Sonia Halliday Photographs; 214, Ronald Sheridan's Photo Library; 215, Michael Holford; 216, Giraudon, Paris.

INDEX

Pages numbered in *italics* refer to the illustrations.